LITERARY MASTERS

ISSN 1526-1530

LITERARY
MASTERS

Volume **9**

Maxine Hong Kingston

Deborah Madsen
South Bank University-London

A MANLY, INC. BOOK

GALE GROUP

Detroit
New York
San Francisco
London
Boston
Woodbridge, CT

MAXINE HONG KINGSTON

Matthew J. Bruccoli and Richard Layman, *Editorial Directors*

The Gale Group

27500 Drake Road

Farmington Hills, MI 48331

ISBN 0-7876-5135-4

ISSN 1526-1530

Printed in the United States of America

10 9 8 7 6 5 4 3 2 1

ADVISORY BOARD

Matthew J. Bruccoli
    Jefferies Professor of English
    University of South Carolina

Denis Donoghue
    Henry James Professor of English and American Letters
    New York University

George Garrett
    Henry Hoyns Professor of Creative Writing
    University of Virginia

Trudier Harris
    J. Carlyle Sitterson Professor of English
    University of North Carolina at Chapel Hill

Hugh Kenner
    Franklin Professor and Callaway Professor
    University of Georgia

Alvin Kernan
    Senior Advisor in the Humanities
    The Andrew W. Mellon Foundation

Richard Layman
    Vice President
    Bruccoli Clark Layman

R.W.B. Lewis
    Neil Grey Professor, Emeritus
    Yale University

Harrison Meserole
    Distinguished Professor of English, Emeritus
    Texas A & M University

TABLE OF CONTENTS

MAXINE HONG KINGSTON

A NOTE TO THE READER

THE TELLER IN THE TALE

by Alvin Kernan,
Senior Advisor in
the Humanities,
The Andrew W.
Mellon Foundation

A few years ago it was fashionable to speak of "the death of the author" and to argue that "language writes, not the man." These postmodernist views were part of a philosophy that discounted the individuality of the writer in favor of a world of impersonal texts and systems, such as language, which furnish a "scriptor" with the only conceptions of reality he or she can have. In this view of things the author disappeared into a "mere grammatical subject"; the time and place were doing the writing, not the author.

This vast, gray, impersonal view has not prevailed, however, because it goes against the grain of what we all know and feel to be the actual case. Historically, our literature is not just a set of coded texts but living writings intertwined with the names of the men and women who wrote them. We cannot think of *The Canterbury Tales* without thinking of the sly but somewhat bumbling Geoffrey Chaucer, good-natured but sharply ironic, who introduces himself as one of the pilgrims in his own poem. And we try our best to see William Shakespeare, always a somewhat mysterious fellow, in the figure of the magician Prospero on his magic island in *The Tempest*. Charles Dickens, as a frightened boy sent to work in the blacking factory in industrialized London, hangs about his novels in the same way that Ernest Hemingway in his macho pose and his death by suicide is always present when we turn the pages of *A Farewell to Arms* or the "Up in Michigan" stories. As in the last example, the lives of the poets often throw dark shadows back on their works. The alcoholic F. Scott Fitzgerald ends his life trying desperately to write another novel as good as his early *The Great Gatsby*. Flannery O'Connor sits in her small house in Georgia, suffering from a disease—lupus—that ravages her immune system, and records experiences of Americans who are as vulnerable to the world as is her own body.

The teller not only writes the tale, but, in doing so, he or she becomes a part of it, and our sense of the tale is not complete until the teller's presence is evoked. This is one reason why biographies and vignettes, collections of biographical information, and memories of the type found in these volumes about our writers are so interesting and so useful. More than useful, really. We have not fully read the tale until we can see the teller in it, who will, if we come to know him or her well enough, sensitize us to how the tale is told and what is likely to be in it. Every tale-teller has a distinctive way of telling—the style—and a particular subject matter. To know who is writing is, therefore, to know to look for things that would otherwise escape us. Theodore Dreiser, the American novelist, was a moody man, pessimistic about the possibilities of life, convinced that our fates are woven from a host of small details, the need for a winter coat in *Sister Carrie* or the bright attractiveness of an upper-middle-class parlor in *An American Tragedy*. These ordinary details can in their bulk bore us and turn us away from the story if we are not aware that this is the Dreiserian signature, the way in which he renders the flatness of ordinary life and points to the fate that lies concealed in it.

Every author differs from every other in how and what he or she writes, but in the end they combine, if we see and know them well enough, to create a scene that is close to the center of literature, to its place and role in the world. Some writing careers portray this scene more powerfully than others do. Samuel Johnson, for example, was a personality so titanic as nearly to overwhelm his writings, physically grotesque, frequently nearly mad with depression, an impoverished hack most of his life, endlessly talking for victory and heroically facing the hard facts of human life. In Johnson's life, writing his great dictionary of the English language or his *Lives of the Poets* was his defense against the madness of emptiness and meaninglessness. That is to say, he wrote to preserve his sanity by giving order and meaning to the world and to the language through which we approach it.

Every teller of tales, when we come to know him or her, is engaged in something like this Johnsonian struggle to order and make sense of the world of random facts and experiences, to preserve some sense of things, people, and times that would otherwise be forgotten and lost forever in the past. Consider another writer, our own Southern novelist William Faulkner, a struggler who is not as successful as Johnson in his authorial task of imposing order on a messy and painful sense of the confusions of life. Faulkner's story is that of a mythical Mississippi county, Yoknapatawpha County, that he creates in an attempt to locate and order in time and space the confused and confusing memories of the

Southern past, such as the Civil War and slavery and primitive wilderness, with modern-day consciousness that cannot forget the past but also cannot reconcile it with its own immediate interests and thoughts. The strain shows in Faulkner's stories, in the absence of clear chronology, in the tangled syntax of his long sentences, in his frequent descent into stream-of-consciousness writing.

To include the tellers with their tales, which is what this series of the Gale Study Guides is designed to make possible for the common reader, is to see the heroic scene of literature itself, throughout the world, where men and women writers make and have made the most skillful use of the word-hoard of language and the freedom of fiction to preserve our collective past and to make sense out of things that in their multitude are always threatening to fly apart into chaos.

ACKNOWLEDGMENTS

This book was produced by Manly, Inc. R. Bland Lawson is the series editor and in-house editor.

Production manager is Philip B. Dematteis.

Copyediting supervisor is Phyllis A. Avant. The copyediting staff includes Brenda Carol Blanton, Melissa D. Hinton, William Tobias Mathes, Jennifer S. Reid, Nancy E. Smith, and Elizabeth Jo Ann Sumner.

The index was prepared by Alex Snead.

Layout and graphics series leader is Karla Corley Brown. She was assisted by Zoe R. Cook and Janet E. Hill, graphics supervisor.

Permissions editor is Jeff Miller.

Photography editors are Charles Mims, Scott Nemzek, and Paul Talbot. Digital photographic copy work was performed by Joseph M. Bruccoli, Zoe R. Cook, and Abraham Richard Layman.

Systems manager is Marie L. Parker.

Typesetting supervisor is Kathleen M. Flanagan. The typesetting staff includes Sarah Mathes, Mark J. McEwan, Patricia Flanagan Salisbury, and Alison Smith.

Following is a list of the copyright holders who have granted us permission to reproduce material in this volume of Gale Study Guides to Great Literature. Every effort has been made to trace copyright, but if omissions have been made, please let us know.

COPYRIGHTED MATERIAL IN *Literary Masters, Vol. 9: Maxine Hong Kingston,* **WAS REPRODUCED FROM THE FOLLOWING SOURCES:**

Maxine Hong Kingston. "Cultural Mis-readings by American Reviewers." In *Asian and Western Writers in Dialogue,* edited by Guy Amirthanayagam. London: Macmillan, 1982.

Maxine Hong Kingston. "Personal Statement." In *Approaches to Teaching the Woman Warrior,* edited by Shirley Geok-lin Lim. New York: Modern Language Association, 1991.

Maxine Hong Kingston. "Useful Education." In *Hawai'i One Summer.* Honolulu: University of Hawaii Press, 1998.

Donna Perry. "Maxine Hong Kingston." In *Backtalk: Women Writers Speak Out, Interviews by Donna Perry* .New Brunswick, N.J.: Rutgers University Press, 1993.

Paula Rabinowitz. "Eccentric Memories: A Conversation With Maxine Hong Kingston." *Michigan Quarterly Review,* 26 (1987): 177–179.

Neila C. Seshachari. "Reinventing Peace: Conversations with Tripmaster Maxine Hong Kingston." *Weber Studies: An Interdisciplinary Humanities Journal,* 12 (Winter 1995): 7–26.

Diane Simmons. *Maxine Hong Kingston.* New York: Twayne, 1999.

Phyllis Hoge Thompson. "This is the Story I Heard: A Conversation with Maxine Hong Kingston and Earll Kingston." *Biography,* 6, no. 1 (1983): 4.

Man with two children, Chinatown. California Historical Society, San Francisco.

Manuscript page from an early draft of *The Woman Warrior.* Courtesy of the Bancroft Library, University of California, Berkeley.

Manuscript page from an early draft of *Tripmaster Monkey.* Courtesy of the Bancroft Library, University of California, Berkeley.

Members of the National Organization for Women demonstrating at the White House.

Students protesting at the University of California, Berkeley, 1964.

Typescript page of *China Men.* Courtesy of Maxine Hong Kingston.

CHRONOLOGY

1940: Maxine Ting Ting Hong is born on 27 October in Stockton, California, to Chinese immigrants, Tom Hong and Ying Lan Chew Hong. She is the first of the couple's six children born in the United States. (Two children born earlier died in China.)

1954–1958: Kingston attends Edison High School in Stockton. In 1955 her essay "I Am an American" is published in *The American Girl,* the magazine of the Girl Scouts, winning her a $5 prize.

1958–1962: Kingston wins a journalism scholarship to the University of California, Berkeley, where she majors at first in engineering but later changes her course of study to English. While attending the university she works on the student newspaper, *The Daily Californian.* She graduates with a B.A. in English in 1962 and on 23 November of that year marries the actor Earll Kingston. 1964: Kingston's son, Joseph Lawrence Chung Mei Kingston, is born.

1964–1965: Kingston studies for a teaching certificate at the University of California, Berkeley, and works as a student teacher at Oakland Technical High School.

1965–1967: Kingston teaches English and mathematics at Sunset High School in Hayward, California. She is active in the protest movement against the Vietnam War.

1967: Kingston moves with her husband and son to Hawaii, where she teaches English at Kahuku High School in Kahuku.

1968: Kingston teaches at Kahaluu Drop-in School in Kahaluu, Hawaii.

1969: Kingston teaches English as a second language at Honolulu Business College and language arts at Kailua High School in Kailua.

1970–1977: Kingston teaches language arts at the Mid-Pacific Institute in Honolulu. In 1976 her first book, *The Woman Warrior: Memoirs of a Girlhood Among Ghosts,* is published by Knopf and wins the National

Book Critics Circle Award for nonfiction. Kingston's short story "Duck Boy" is published in the 12 June 1977 issue of *The New York Times Magazine*.

1977–1981: Kingston is a visiting professor of English at the University of Hawaii in Honolulu.

1980: Kingston's *China Men* is published by Knopf and is named to the American Library Association Notable Books List. She is named a "Living Treasure of Hawaii" by a Honolulu Buddhist sect.

1981: *China Men* wins the National Book Award for nonfiction, is nominated for a National Book Critics Circle Award, and is a finalist for the Pulitzer Prize in nonfiction. The Bancroft Library at the University of California, Berkeley, begins to compile the Maxine Hong Kingston Papers as one of its special collections.

1982: Kingston tours Japan, Australia, Indonesia, Malaysia, and Hong Kong on a trip sponsored by the United States International Communication Agency and the Adelaide Arts Festival in Australia.

1984: Kingston visits China for the first time with a group of six other writers—Allen Ginsberg, Gary Snyder, Francine du Plessix Gray, Leslie Marmon Silko, Toni Morrison, and Harrison Salisbury—on a tour sponsored by the University of California, Los Angeles, and the Chinese Writers Association. Kingston moves with her husband from Hawaii to Los Angeles; their son, Joseph, remains in Hawaii, where he has established himself as a musician.

1986: Kingston is named Thelma McAndless Distinguished Professor in the Humanities at Eastern Michigan University.

1987: Kingston's *Hawai'i One Summer, 1978* is published by Meadow Press in a limited edition of two hundred copies. *Through the Black Curtain,* comprising excerpts from *The Woman Warrior, China Men,* and the manuscript of her novel-in-progress, "Tripmaster Monkey," is published by the Friends of the Bancroft Library at the University of California, Berkeley. She moves with her husband to Oakland, California.

1989: Kingston's first novel, *Tripmaster Monkey: His Fake Book,* is published by Knopf and wins the PEN/USA West Award for fiction. In November she spends a week at the University of California, Santa Cruz, as a University of California Regents Lecturer.

1990: Kingston is appointed a Chancellor's Distinguished Professor in the English department at the University of California, Berkeley. The television program *Maxine Hong Kingston: Talking Story* is produced by Joan Saffa and Stephen Talbot for the Public Broadcasting System station KQED in San Francisco and CrossCurrent Media.

1991: Kingston gives the Martha Heasley Cox Lecture at San Jose State University. In October the Kingstons' home is destroyed in an Oakland Hills fire, along with all of Kingston's manuscripts, including a novel-in-progress, provisionally titled "The Book of Peace" or "The Fourth Book of Peace." She begins work on another manuscript, to be called "The Fifth Book of Peace."

1992: Kingston receives a fellowship from the Lila Wallace Reader's Digest Fund and uses the prize money to begin writing workshops for veterans of the Vietnam War. She is inducted into the American Academy of Arts and Sciences.

1993: On a leave of absence from teaching at the University of California, Berkeley, Kingston holds a series of workshops, "A Time to Be: Reflective Writing, Mindfulness, and the War: A Time for Veterans and their Families," through the Community for Mindful Living in Berkeley.

1994: Kingston acts as guest conductor for a benefit concert with the Berkeley Symphony Orchestra. A dramatized version of *The Woman Warrior* is produced and performed by the Berkeley Repertory Theatre and, later in the year, by the Huntington Theatre Company at Boston University.

1995: Kingston participates in a conference, "Vietnam Legacies: Twenty Years Later," at the University of California, Davis. The stage adaptation of *The Woman Warrior* is produced by the Center Theatre Group of Los Angeles.

1997: Kingston returns to teaching at the University of California, Berkeley, and participates in a conference, "Peacemaking: The Power of Nonviolence," held in San Francisco in June. In September she is presented with a National Humanities Medal by President Bill Clinton.

1998: Kingston wins the John Dos Passos Prize for Literature for *Tripmaster Monkey.*

ABOUT MAXINE HONG KINGSTON

Born: 27 October 1940 in Stockton, California

Married: Earll Kingston, 23 November 1962

Education: Edison High School, Stockton, and the University of California, Berkeley

CHILDHOOD AND BIOGRAPHICAL GLIMPSES

Maxine Hong Kingston's first two books, *The Woman Warrior: Memoirs of a Girlhood Among Ghosts* (1976) and *China Men* (1980), are routinely referred to as works of autobiography. She would seem to have lent her authority to this view by the subtitle she gave to *The Woman Warrior*. But she describes her initial sense of all her work as that of a novelist, and she ascribes the decision to call her first two books nonfiction to her editors, who told her that reviewers are reluctant to review first novels, while readers feel they can identify with the people and narrative of an autobiography or memoir. Yet, all of Kingston's work to date reveals a close affinity with the events and people of her own life. In *The Woman Warrior* she relates incidents from her childhood and early life; in *China Men* she writes about the immigrant history that produced her; and in her first novel, *Tripmaster Monkey: His Fake Book* (1989), she draws on events from the years she attended the University of California, Berkeley.

Kingston was born Maxine Ting Ting Hong on 27 October 1940 in Stockton, California, the oldest child of Tom Hong and Ying Lan Chew Hong, immigrants from southern China. (Two children born to the Hongs before they immigrated died in China.) Her parents came from the village of Sun Woi, near Canton (Guangzhou), and were unusually literate and highly educated. Kingston recalls that they would recite classic Chinese poetry as well as village songs and rhymes and that as a young girl she failed to appreciate the extent of their learning. She describes her father as a poet, though she does not come from a family of writers. She

Maxine Hong Kingston in 1993

explains, "I feel I come from a tradition of literate people, even though they weren't writers."[1]

Kingston's father immigrated to the United States in 1924. In China he had been a scholar and teacher, but when he arrived in New York City he was compelled to find manual rather than intellectual work. Fifteen years passed before he was able to send for his wife. During that time Ying Lan (Brave Orchid) studied medicine and worked as a doctor. Tom Hong eventually established a laundry in New York with two friends. When he found himself cheated of his proper share of the business, he moved with his wife, who had by then joined him, to Stockton. Here he initially worked as the manager of a gambling house, taking the owner's place when the police raided and arrested everybody. In *China Men* Kingston relates the story of how she was named. According to her mother, her father named her "after a blonde gambler who always won" because he considered it a "lucky American name."[2] Kingston also describes the difficult circumstances in which her parents bought their house in Stockton. Twice they found a house they wished to buy, but in both cases the gambling-house owner, whom they asked to handle the transaction because he spoke English, bought the place himself and rented it to the Hongs, thus keeping them in the position of tenants. After finding a third house, Kingston's parents said nothing to the gambling-house owner about their intentions until they had paid for it themselves—in cash. Kingston recalls that "It was exactly like the owner's house, the same size, the same floor plan and gingerbread. . . . It was the biggest but most run-down of the houses; it had been a boarding house for old China Men. Rose bushes with thorns grew around it, wooden lace hung broken from the porch eaves, the top step was missing like a moat. The rooms echoed" (246). After the gambling house closed, the Hongs operated the New Port Laundry on El Dorado Street in Stockton.

All the family, including the children, shared the hard work of running the laundry. Here Kingston listened to her parents and other relatives "talk-story" as they recalled Chinese myths, fables, and history. In her writing she uses the stories she remembers from her childhood, and her memory helps to filter the important and enduring stories from the less significant: "I wrote from stories I remembered, because I knew if I asked them [her parents] again, they would just tell another version. Besides, I feel that what is remembered is very important. The mind selects out images and facts that have a certain significance. If I remember something that someone told me 20 years ago, then the story has lasted in that form for a very long time."[3]

While Kingston admits to feeling that she is a "West Coast Chinese American," she identifies with the rural country of the Central California Valley, "Stockton, Sacramento, Fresno, all of the Valley in the north," rather than the city of San Francisco.[4] In *The Woman Warrior* she gives a few glimpses of the Stockton in which she grew up. She refers to the time when "urban renewal tore down my parents' laundry and paved over our slum for a parking lot. . . ."[5] The Chinatown Kingston grew up in was located in the area surrounding Lafayette Street but was destroyed to make way for a crosstown freeway. About the destruction, she says, "our Chinatown was just a block and then the freeway wiped it out. It was such an insult, because they didn't finish the freeway. They just made it go through Chinatown and it stopped right there."[6] The freeway remained incomplete for years, and its lack of purpose, coupled with the destruction that had made its partial construction possible, engendered what Kingston describes as paranoia among the residents. But she also admits that the destruction of the physical area that was Chinatown made her realize that the community existed not in a particular place but in the rituals and memories that everyone shared.

The Hong family lived in a rough neighborhood. In *The Woman Warrior* Kingston describes how her mother "locked her children in the house so we couldn't look at dead slum people" (51). When Brave Orchid showed her sister around Stockton, she advised her how to avoid Skid Row on days when she was not feeling strong: "On days when you are not feeling safe, walk around it. But you can walk through it unharmed on your strong days" (139). In *China Men* Kingston recalls the derelicts and drunkards who tormented the children, telling of an afternoon when her sister barricaded herself under the dining-room table to escape the wino who was knocking on all the doors and windows (180). Their house was located adjacent to the railroad, a constant reminder of her great-grandfather's contribution to the building of the transcontinental railroad. In describing the funeral of a great-uncle, Kau Goong, Kingston tells of how the procession headed for the Chinese cemetery and traveled past all the places that Kau Goong frequented in life, so that his ghost would not settle in any of these places: the Hongs' house, Kau Goong's club, the Benevolent Association in Chinatown, the Chinese school, the Catholic church, stores, and the laundry. Her fiction is based in this environment.

Kingston attended the Chung Wah Chinese School for Chinese American children on East Church Street in Stockton. In classes lasting from five o'clock to eight o'clock every night and from nine o'clock until noon on Sundays the children were taught how to write and speak Chi-

Maxine Ting Ting Hong Kingston is a graduate of the University of California at Berkeley. She lives in Honolulu with her husband and small son, and teaches English and creative writing at a private school there. *The Woman Warrior* is her first book.

Dust jacket of Kingston's first book, published in 1976, a collection of tales based on her childhood and family history

nese. In *The Woman Warrior* Kingston draws a series of contrasts between the American and Chinese schools, noting the different attitudes of the teachers and the children who would not speak English at the American school but did speak Chinese at the Chinese school. In *Hawai'i One Summer* (1987) she recalls her days at Edison High School, remembering that she had black girlfriends in school but was not really of their "set." She did not consider sitting anywhere but at the Chinese lunch table: "There were more of us than places at that table. Hurry and get to the cafeteria early, or go late when somebody may have finished and left a seat."[7] The experience of being enmeshed in the Chinese community of Stockton provided the basis for Kingston's writing. As a writer, she has been particularly affected by her recollection of the demands made by the two languages in which she was schooled as a child: English and the Chinese dialect spoken by her parents.

Kingston's parents, like most of the Chinese community in Stockton at that time, came from the Say Yup region of China; the dialect of Cantonese known as "Say Yup" was Kingston's first language. This has posed problems for her because the dialect has no written form. Even if she could represent these Chinese words and concepts in the alphabet of the English language, it would not satisfy her aim of representing the

KINGSTON ON DIALECT

"I encourage my own students to write in dialect, and give them [poet] Lew Welch's instructions on how to do it: 'Dialect is only a regional and personal voiceprint.... You can easily separate structure and meaning from dialect, and still be dealing with sound, with music, with speech, with another's Mind. Gertrude Stein perfectly mimicked the rhythms and structures of Baltimore Blacks in her story "Melanctha" and she didn't transcribe the dialect at all—that is, didn't have to misspell a lot of words to get the work done. Nelson Algren has many many passages with no misspellings, but he catches the real flow of regional speech.'"

Maxine Hong Kingston

From "Lew Welch: An Appreciation," in *Hawai'i One Summer* (Honolulu: University of Hawaii Press, 1998), p. 65.

words spoken by Chinese Americans with an American accent. As Kingston has explained, "I'm specifically interested in how the Chinese American dialect is spoken in the California Valley. . . . When I write dialogue for people who are speaking Chinese, I say the words to myself in Chinese and then write them in English, hoping to capture some of the sounds and rhythms and power of Say Yup."[8]

Language caused Kingston difficulties especially in her first years at school when, not knowing English and suffering fear and shyness as a result, she withdrew into silence. (This retreat into silence still comes upon the adult Kingston from time to time.) During such periods in her childhood she communicated in pictures rather than words, and for a time after she finished college she considered that perhaps she should work as a painter rather than a writer. Her awareness that she had in a sense already served her apprenticeship with words, whereas she was only beginning to learn the skills of a painter, took her back to writing.

Kingston began writing at the age of eight or nine, and indeed describes herself as a "born writer," someone who cannot *not* write: her life has been shaped by what she calls "this desire always to find the words for life and for the invisible and for the visible and for the imagination."[9] Even when she was experiencing difficulty speaking, she continued to write. Kingston has described her memory of the first time a poem came to her: "I was sitting in a class and all of a sudden this poem came to me. I wrote 25 verses in something like a trance. I don't recall what the class was about."[10] All through high school she wrote stories rather than poetry and confesses that the inability to understand the form of the academic essay or assignment meant that she received some poor grades. She recalls clearing space in her parents' stockroom for her papers and notes. The stories she wrote in high school were to become those that make up *The Woman Warrior* and *China Men*. Kingston wrote these stories in various forms, with each successive version revealing her increased maturity and skill as a writer. For example, she explains how she "tried telling the *China Men* stories like Jason and the Argonauts, because I read that as a kid, where they were using epic hexameter meter, and so I tried to tell the story of the China Men as Jason and the quest for the Golden Fleece, using the hexameter rhythms and epic form. I suppose for decades I kept telling the same stories again and again, but each time I told it I had a better vocabulary and better craft."[11]

The literary influences upon Kingston's work, especially her early work, are limited. Kingston describes her childhood reading as being much like any other child's. However, Jade Snow Wong's *Fifth Chinese Daughter* (1945) had a significant impact upon her. In this autobiographical work, which is narrated by a young girl, Kingston found a Chinese American character with whom she could identify. At this point she realized that she had been falsely identifying with, and attempting to write stories about, the Caucasian characters with whom she was familiar from her reading. Kingston tells of a similar moment of self-consciousness while reading Louisa May Alcott's *Little Women* (1868): "I was reading along, identifying with the March sisters, when I came across this funny-looking little Chinaman. It popped out of the book. I'd been pushed into my place. I was him, I wasn't those March girls."[12] This kind of experience of exclusion from mainstream literature motivated her to create for herself a place in literature. Beyond this initial inspiration, her parents' stock of myths, histories, and stories inspired and shaped her writing. Kingston reads a great deal of poetry, especially modern American poetry, and the work of prose writers such as Grace Paley and Cynthia Ozick who write in a poetic style. Virginia Woolf's writing, in particular her novel *Orlando* (1928), has influenced aspects of Kingston's work, as she has explained: "I do some of the same tricks with time like the China Men who have lived for hundreds of years, just like Orlando lived for hundreds of years, and their history goes on and on."[13] Two other writers who stand out as having had an important impact upon Kingston's work are William Carlos Williams and Walt Whitman. The influence of Whitman is most clearly seen in *Tripmaster Monkey*, in which the protagonist takes the name Wittman Ah Sing, echoing several poems in the 1881–1882 edition of Whitman's *Leaves of Grass*, such as "One's-Self I Sing."

KINGSTON ON WRITING HER FIRST POEM

"I was supposed to have been writing the multiplication tables or making our daily copy of the map of California. We had to draw every squiggle in the coastline. How lucky the fourth graders in Colorado are, we said. Instead I wrote down the music and the voices I heard. So, as a teacher, when I see students staring at nothing, I am loathe to interrupt."

Maxine Hong Kingston

From "Useful Education," in *Hawai'i One Summer* (Honolulu: University of Hawaii Press, 1998), pp. 42–43.

Kingston acknowledges Williams's essay collection *In the American Grain* (1925) as an early influence, especially the way in which he retold the myth of America. In his re-creation of the origin of the nation—telling the story of how it came into being—she perceives a profound connection between his work and her own, especially *China Men*. Kingston points to the coincidence that the earliest episode in her book takes place around 1850, which is the historical end point of Williams's book. Both writers tried to achieve a poetic retelling of American history. In *China Men* Kingston inserts almost as a halfway marker in the narrative a factual history of Chinese Americans, beginning with the California gold rush of the late 1840s and continuing through the various discriminatory acts of legislation that have helped to define the Chinese experience in America. She departed from her usual indirect style to write this chronological history because she was frustrated by the lack of awareness of Chinese American history among her readership. She could not simply assume that her readers would know the historical background to which she referred. Thus, Kingston filled in those gaps in the historical knowledge of her audience, hoping that "maybe another Chinese American author won't have to write that history."[14]

Kingston invokes this sense of claiming a place for Chinese Americans in the history of the United States when she describes her work as "claiming America."[15] She does not mean that Asian people should simply accept American values and lifestyles; rather, she means that Asian Americans belong to the nation as a part of its history and diverse culture and are not "outsiders" existing only on the margins of American life. As Kingston points out in her discussion of the role of Chinese laborers in the construction of the transcontinental railroad, without Chinese Americans, the United States would be a quite different country from what it is today. For this reason the grandfathers in *China Men* are not given personal names; they are called "great-grandfather" and "great-great-grandfather" because they then can take on a kind of mythological stature as the great-grandfathers of the nation. Kingston's writing is always about America rather than China; her effort is to reveal and celebrate the place of the Chinese in American history and culture and to have that contribution recognized. In addition, she is forging a place for Chinese American writers in the tradition of American literature. She recalls that when she wrote the story of the No Name Woman, the first story in *The Woman Warrior,* she was thinking of Nathaniel Hawthorne's depiction of the adulterous Hester Prynne in *The Scarlet Letter* (1850). The title of "The Making of More Americans," from *China Men,* deliberately echoes Gertrude Stein's *The Making of Americans* (1925), in which Stein attempted to forge a new American language, though Kingston has worked to create an American language with Chinese accents. In this way she responds to the social, political, and also literary exclusion of Chinese Americans from the mainstream of American life and culture.

Maxine and Earll Kingston, whom she married in 1962, moved from Berkeley to Hawaii in 1967. The reason for the move she describes as primarily an attempt to discover an answer to the question "Is there life after Berkeley?"[16] Despite the antiwar efforts in which the Kingstons and their friends in Berkeley participated, the Vietnam War continued unabated. The disappointment this caused her and her husband, combined with the effect of the drug culture on friends whom she describes as "burned out," prompted them to seek an alternative lifestyle. En route to their original destination, the Far East, they stopped in Hawaii and stayed for seventeen years, returning to California in 1984. In 1967 Hawaii brought the reality of the war in Indochina closer than the Kingstons had experienced it in Berkeley. Kingston recalls, "Hawaii had its own problems, and with the presence of the military here, the Vietnam War was even more real on these islands."[17] Hawaii was militarized in ways that California was not; troops passed through the islands on their way to Vietnam, and veterans came to Hawaii for R and R ("Rest and Recreation") between tours of duty. Both Kingston and her husband worked with veterans, at a church sanctuary for soldiers who were AWOL, and she learned from them that not everyone shared the antiwar sentiments of her friends and colleagues in Berkeley. These soldiers were not necessarily absent without leave because they objected to the war: some did not like the conditions under which they served, some disliked their officers or the food, and some were just fooling around, according to Kingston. In *Hawai'i One Summer* she recalls one young soldier in particular. In answer to her question about the things he likes to do, he tells her, "'I build model cars. . . . I built five hundred of them,

IDENTIFYING WITH CHARACTERS

"Stop the music—I have to butt in and introduce myself and my race. 'Dear reader, all these characters whom you've been identifying with—Bill, Brooke, and Annie—are Chinese—and I am too.' The fiction is spoiled. You who read have been suckered along, identifying like hell, only to find out that you'd been getting a peculiar, colored, slanted p.o.v. 'Call me Ishmael.' See? You pictured a white guy, didn't you? If Ishmael were described—ochery ecru amber umber skin—you picture a tan white guy. Wittman wanted to spoil those stories coming out of and set in New England Back East—to blacken and to yellow Bill, Brooke, and Annie. A new rule for the imagination: The common man has Chinese looks. From now on, whenever you read about those people with no surnames, color them with black skin or yellow skin."

Maxine Hong Kingston

From *Tripmaster Monkey: His Fake Book* (New York: Knopf, 1989), p. 34.

HAWAII: U.S. SOLDIERS ON LEAVE FROM VIETNAM

"Many of the soldiers had not been wounded in Vietnam but in auto accidents here, bike accidents, swimming and surfing accidents; also they shot one another. Once out of Vietnam, they got careless, sucked through the Blowhole, drowned in the lagoons, swept away in the undertows, killed the first day or week out of Vietnam. Beaten up by locals. 'Swim out there,' the girls said, practicing their siren ways, pointing to the Witch's Brew, the Potato Patch, the Toilet."

Maxine Hong Kingston

From "War," in *Hawai'i One Summer* (Honolulu: University of Hawaii Press, 1998), p. 17.

and I lined 'em up and shot 'em and set 'em on fire.' 'Why did you do that?' 'It felt good—like when I was a door gunner on the chopper in Nam. Thousands of bullets streaming out of my gun.'" Silently she replies, "Don't tell me about the gooks you shot, I thought. Don't tell me about the hootches you torched" (18–19).

War and martial conflict feature prominently in Kingston's first two books, though she writes in order to discover a way to overcome difference and hostility without violence. The decision to use *The Woman Warrior* as the title of her first book was made by her editor, and Kingston has come to regret it. In emphasizing a martial image of women, the title suggests that war may be a way of resolving issues, whereas Kingston has always been motivated by her pacifist ideals and the quest for nonviolent means of resolving conflicts. She remarks, "I keep hoping we will all take the woman warrior in another sense, that there are other ways to fight wars than with swords."[18] This concern with how peace may be possible has affected not only her writing but also her life, first with her antiwar activities and later with her involvement in the antidraft movement in Hawaii: "It's as if my writing spilled over into real life, and I felt I had to act. It's not that I enjoy it. Anti-draft [*sic*] work intrudes on my life, so I just put my resentment right back into the struggle. I don't like going to meetings or carrying signs, but I feel that it is my duty."[19]

Kingston has remarked that Hawaii is not an easy place to feel a part of: "I think this is a hard place to belong to."[20] But Hawaii has embraced her; in 1980, shortly after the publication of *China Men*, she was honored as a Living Treasure of Hawaii by a Buddhist sect in Honolulu. The ceremony followed a tradition that was brought to Hawaii from ancient China, via modern Japan. Kingston explains that "in the same way that we designate paintings and monuments and mountains as treasures, they designate certain people as Living Treasures."[21] At age thirty-nine she was unusually young to receive this honor; she was also the first Chinese American to be honored in this way. At the same time the designation underscored her own feeling of not really belonging to Hawaii. The tradition itself represents a strategy used by the Buddhist priests to make themselves a part of the culture of Hawaii: "They decided that one way was to honor some of Hawaii's treasures. It makes me feel really good to be honored by them. It feels as if the islands are saying, 'You can be a part of Hawaii too.'"[22]

Kingston's teaching experiences, first in California and then in Hawaii, have had a lasting influence upon the way in which she views her audience—both her readers and those who attend her readings. She does not assume that she has a particular kind of readership and does not address herself to an exclusively Chinese American or Asian American audience. Rather, she tries to take everybody into account, calling herself a "megalomaniac" in this respect: "Everybody living today and people in the future, that's my audience, for generations."[23]

KINGSTON ON TEACHING AND WRITING

"I have taught school for twelve years. I've taught grammar school, high school, alternative school, business school, and college; math, English, English as a second language, journalism, and creative writing. I've also been a writer for twenty-eight years, the writing years and the teaching years overlapping. I ought to be able to tell how to teach people to write."

Maxine Hong Kingston

From "Useful Education," in *Hawai'i One Summer* (Honolulu: University of Hawaii Press, 1998), p. 41.

In Kingston's childhood and upbringing there were obvious cultural factors that influenced the nature of her subsequent work: particularly her awareness of the position of women in Chinese culture, her experience of American racism, and her sense of a cross-cultural identity. She says that she is a feminist because of the upbringing she had: "Growing up as a kid, I don't see how I could not have been a feminist. In Chinese culture, people always talk about how girls are bad."[24] Many of the stories in *The Woman Warrior* were motivated by feminist anger and vision.[25] For example, Kingston recalls the anger she felt when her mother first told her the story of her father's sister, the woman whose life is the subject of "No Name Woman": "I was so mad at my mother for telling me a cruel tale for the joy of the telling."[26] Later she saw how the battle against silence in "No Name Woman" relates to her mother's instruction that she must never repeat the story. Kingston has also broken the silence surrounding the misogynistic traditions that express the patriarchal character of Chinese society. These traditions include the institutionalized servitude of women through practices such as female infanticide, infant betrothal, female slavery, concubinage, and prostitution. Gender relations are organized according to Confucian patriarchy, which means that women are obedient to the men in their family and derive their identity from the family; marriage is both a woman's life and her fate.

Children playing in San Francisco's Chinatown, photographed circa 1895–1906 by the German-born Arnold Genthe. In 1978 Kingston wrote about Genthe's pictures for *American Heritage:* "We see . . . groups of children playing—the wonderful picture of the row of children . . . holding on to one another's pigtails—and this gives the impression that Chinatown was a healthy community of flourishing families when exactly the opposite was the actual, lonely situation."

Confucian patriarchy not only organizes social relations according to gender but also gives the Chinese language a powerful gender inflection. In both *The Woman Warrior* and *China Men* Kingston recalls with outrage the degrading proverbs she heard as a child: "Girls are maggots in the rice" (43) and "It is more profitable to raise geese than daughters" (46) The Chinese language embodies the assumption of feminine inferiority; in *The Woman Warrior* she observes, "There is a Chinese word for the female I—which is 'slave'. Break the women with their own tongues!" (47). The terms "girl" and "bad" are used as if they are synonymous: "'I'm not a bad girl,' I would scream. . . . I might as well have said, 'I'm not a girl'" (46). Kingston also recalls the words she heard that were reserved for girls, such as "pig" and "stink pig" (204).

Kingston's awareness of Chinese history and of the generational differences between herself and her parents has been deeply influenced by gender issues. In *The Woman Warrior* she muses on the transformation of Chinese society effected by the Communist Revolution, which "put an end to prostitution by giving women what they wanted: a job and a room of their own" (62). Nonetheless, she shared her parents' perception that poverty was still endemic in China. The Revolution changed attitudes and cultural practices to the extent that it enabled Kingston's mother to become educated, but still she owned a female slave (a *mui tsai*). Brave Orchid was a contradictory character: she tried to raise her daughter in the traditional Chinese fashion of submissiveness and subordination, but she was herself a forceful and opinionated woman, fiercely independent and strong-willed.

In *China Men* Kingston continues to explore the issues of misogyny but within the context of feminine self-oppression: situations in which women insist upon the practice of traditions that oppress other women. In the story "On Discovery," for example, it is a group of women, not men, who transform the traveler Tang Ao into a powerless woman by breaking his toes and binding his feet, thus mutilating his body according to patriarchal ritual. In "The Father from China" Kingston's paternal grandmother, Ah Po, demonstrates the feminine internalization of misogynistic values in an episode in which her husband, Ah Goong, swaps his son for a daughter. She insists that the girl be returned and her son retrieved, shouting that her husband must be insane to have swapped a boy for a slave. The neighbors agree with Ah Po's estimation: they would have sold the girl to Ah Goong if only he had asked, and when Ah Po accuses them of cheating her foolish husband and trying to swindle him, they simply hang their heads in shame. Kingston wonders if this experience accounts in part for her father's behavior and for the woman-hating obscenities he mutters when he is angry. Ah Po herself is no weak woman: she is "a woman six feet tall on toy feet" (21), formidably strong and capable, yet she acts to maintain the inferior status of women. Ah Po is a woman of the same type as her daughter-in-law, Brave Orchid. In "The American Father" Kingston describes the depression her father (called "BaBa") experiences after the gambling house has closed and he is out of work. BaBa's decline is attributed to his loss of status. He has become a "slave" (that is, like a woman) and he is outstripped by his wife: "Her energy slammed BaBa back into his chair. She took over everything; he did not have a reason to get up" (250).

The radical gender division that Kingston was taught as a child resulted in her inability to understand that men and women are equally human. In "The American Father" she questions whether boys actually have feelings and can experience pain: "Girls and women of all races cried and had feelings. We had to toughen up. We had to be as tough as boys, tougher because we only pretended not to feel pain" (252). But with the return of her father's spirit comes the "new idea that males have feelings" (254). A parallel is developed between the doomed poet Ch'ü Yüan, whose story is told in "The Li Sao: An Elegy," and BaBa—both live in exile, both have been reduced from high status to no status at all, and both are remembered in stories for their suffering and wisdom. Ch'ü Yüan also offers a symbolic parallel with Kingston's No Name aunt: he represents a male counterpart to her feminine sacrifice. This comparison demonstrates the unequal treatment of the sexes in patriarchal Chinese culture: both Ch'ü Yüan and the No Name aunt overstep the boundaries of authority, but when the poet drowns himself, the people do penance for the injustice they have done him, while the aunt's death is greeted with the further punishment of banishment from family history and communal memory.

Kingston's upbringing within an immigrant Chinese community gave rise to the theme of exclusion in her writing—from Western culture as an Asian and from Chinese culture as a woman. This theme is related to the cross-cultural pressures she represents as an Asian American and her desire to win approval on the terms of both cultures, even when the cultural demands are in conflict. Kingston has tried to understand the conflicting demands made of her by her Chinese ancestry and her American childhood. In her work she is critical of Chinese culture, which belittles her because of her gender (represented most dramatically by her tirade against her mother in "White Tigers," from *The Woman Warrior*). Adopting an American perspective in one story in *The Woman Warrior*, she hears Chinese voices and remarks, "You can see the disgust on American faces looking at women like that. It isn't just the loudness. It is the way Chinese sounds, chingchong ugly, to American ears, not beautiful like Japanese sayonara words with the consonants and vowels as regular as Italian" (171). The effort to analyze and understand the two cultures is difficult but essential; the alternative is represented by Brave Orchid's sister Moon Orchid, who finds the two different lifestyles impossible to reconcile and loses her sanity.

In *The Woman Warrior* Kingston admits to her difficulties in understanding Chinese culture, particularly when so much is unspoken and unexplained: "How can Chinese keep any traditions at all? They don't even make you pay attention, slipping in a ceremony and clearing the table before the children notice specialness. The adults get mad, evasive, and shut you up if you ask" (185). However, she is also aware that she does not belong entirely to American society either. Only by adopting the mythical persona of the woman warrior can she imagine bringing the two cultures together: "Nobody in history has conquered and united both North America and Asia" (49). In *China Men* Kingston confronts the issue of discrimination more openly in terms of racial conflict between Chinese and Anglo-Americans. The chapter titled "The Laws" lists the racist legislation that has limited Asian immigration to the United States. Kingston undermines the stereotypes upon which this legislative prejudice is based by high-lighting the diversity that exists among the Chinese of different regions. She perceives herself as living in a country "where we are eccentric people" (16).

In *China Men* Kingston describes the emasculation of Chinese men who come to America and work in demeaning jobs in the sugar fields of Hawaii, on railroad-construction gangs, and in laundries and restaurants. This powerlessness or "femininity" leads to conflict between Chinese men and women: the men find themselves forced to do demeaning "women's" tasks like laundry work. As her father irons shirts Kingston overhears him mutter curses: "Dog vomit. Your mother's cunt. Your mother's smelly cunt" (12). Her father denies the stories Brave Orchid tells him about her exploitation by the Chinese owner of the gambling house and his family, who treat her—just as they treat him—as their slave. Kingston's father's suffering is expressed by his "wordless male screams that jolted the house upright and staring in the middle of the night" (13), which are matched by his threatening silences. The entire narrative is motivated by her attempts to create a past for her father and an explanation for his behavior, to know that when he utters feminine obscenities "those curses are only common Chinese sayings. That you did not mean to make me sicken at being female" (14). Thus, Kingston issues a challenge to her father: "I tell you what I suppose from your silences and few words, and you can tell me that I'm mistaken. You'll just have to speak up with the real stories if I've got you wrong" (15). As it progresses, the narrative moves to ever wider perspectives in the attempt to reconstruct all the forces that shaped her father's identity and his life.

KINGSTON ON CHINESE CULTURE IN AMERICA

"Do we have a culture that's not these knickknacks we sell to the bok gwai [white devils]? If Chinese-American culture is not knick-knackatory—look at it—backscratcher swizzle sticks, pointed chopsticks for the hair, Jade East aftershave in a Buddha-shape bottle, the head screws off and you pour lotion out of its neck—then what is it? No other people sell out their streets like this. Tourists can't buy up J-town. Wait a goddamn minute. We don't make Jade East. . . . Would we do that to you? Make Jesus-on-the-cross bottles, so every morning, all over the country, hairy men twist his head off, and pour this green stuff out of his neck? So what do we have in the way of a culture besides Chinese hand laundries?"

Maxine Hong Kingston

From *Tripmaster Monkey: His Fake Book* (New York: Knopf, 1989), p. 27.

Revenge is an important component of Chinese culture and Kingston's writing, but she represents vengeance as the accomplishment of justice where before there was exclusion, prejudice, and discrimination based upon both gender and race. This kind of vengeance is based not on violence but on exposing injustice by finding the words with which to represent it accurately and give it artistic shape. The title of *The Woman Warrior* points to the importance of the theme of resistance and rebellion. Various rebellions are interleaved in the text: first, Kingston's rebellion against conventional literary forms, which are inadequate to express her cross-cultural position; second, her rebellion against her powerful mother; and third, her rebellion against the patriarchal Chinese cultural influences to which she was subject. Common to each of these rebellions is Kingston's revolt against imposed racial and gender identities.

Closely related to the idea of achieving vengeance through literary expression is the theme of silence, though the ability of a woman to express herself is related to the motif of mutilation. The woman warrior bears the villagers' wrongs carved into her back. Kingston's mother cuts her daughter's frenum—the connecting membrane under the tongue—for one of two reasons: either to silence her and repress the "ready tongue [that] is an evil tongue" (164), or to free her tongue to learn many languages. Other women in *The Woman Warrior* are afflicted with silence. The No Name aunt gives "silent birth" (11). Kingston bullies and assaults a classmate who refuses to talk. Moon Orchid is unable to talk about her confusion of fantasy with reality and goes mad. Kingston comments, "I thought talking and not talking made the difference between sanity and insanity. Insane people were the ones who couldn't explain themselves" (186). She is haunted by a fear of being thought insane and worries that her parents will betroth her to the retarded boy who visits the laundry. In the final chapter of the book she makes a list of grievances to tell her mother—to make her mutilated tongue work in the cause of her own liberation. In *China Men* Kingston seeks to articulate racial rather than gender prejudice. The narrative attempts to rewrite the history of the United States, to reclaim the role of Chinese labor in the creation of America, and in so doing to reinvent the notion of "the American" to incorporate the Chinese immigrant experience and its cross-cultural legacy. In this way Kingston challenges exclusive definitions of American national identity.

The relationship between *The Woman Warrior* and *China Men* is explained by Kingston's views about feminism as a movement. In the latter book her girl narrator grows up and learns how to tell the story of the men's lives. Kingston explains that in her view feminism must do the same thing: "I believe that in order to truly grow up, women must love men. That has to be the next stage of feminism: I can't think that feminism just breaks off at the point where we get to join the Marines."[27] Originally the two works were to have been one big book but, as Kingston has said, the men's stories interfered with the coherence and unity of the feminine values: the "men's stories seemed to interfere. They were weakening the feminist point of view. So I took all the men's stories out, and then I had *The Woman Warrior*."[28]

AWARDS AND RECOGNITION

The quality of Kingston's work was recognized long before the publication of her widely acclaimed first book. In 1955, at the age of fifteen, she won a $5 prize for her essay "I Am an American," which was published in *The American Girl,* the magazine of the Girl Scouts. When *The Woman Warrior* came out in 1976 it won several prestigious literary prizes. Though the book was published as a work of nonfiction in order to make it more understandable for reviewers and readers, Kingston's editors

Photograph of Kingston that accompanied a review of *China Men* in the 15 June 1980 issue of *The New York Times Book Review*

soon regretted that decision. The book won the National Book Critics Circle Award for nonfiction, but Kingston recalls an editor telephoning her to say that if the book had been published as fiction she would have stood a good chance of winning in the more prestigious fiction category. Charles Elliott, Kingston's editor at Alfred A. Knopf in New York, confesses that he was nervous about her appearance at the awards dinner. After all, the first time she came to his office she was wearing a borrowed coat that was far too big for her and a stocking cap; in Elliott's words, "she looked like a bag lady." At the awards dinner Kingston was the last of four speakers. Elliott continues: "She arrived wearing a dress that came down all the way to the ground and wearing a lei of flowers that were very fragrant. . . . She was so short that she couldn't see over the rostrum and had to bend the microphone over the side to speak. I remember thinking, 'Oh, no!' She had started off with this tiny little voice and before I could believe it, she had it right under absolute control with everyone nearly weeping."[29] The audience was particularly touched, in Elliott's recollection, by Kingston's confession that in thirty years of writing she had never thought of herself as a writer but that, with the presentation of the award, she learned that she was indeed a writer.

In the years immediately following the publication of *The Woman Warrior* Kingston won the *Mademoiselle* Magazine Award and the Anisfield-Wolf Award for Race Relations. Her second book, *China Men*, met with similar acclaim: it was named to the American Library Association Notable Books List in 1980 and won the National Book Award for nonfiction in 1981. It was also nominated for the National Book Critics Circle Award and was a finalist for the Pulitzer Prize in nonfiction. When her first novel, *Tripmaster Monkey*, was published in 1989, it won the PEN/USA West award for fiction.

In recognition of the contribution her writing has made to West Coast and Asian American literature, Kingston received the Stockton Arts Commission Award and the Asian-Pacific Women's Network Woman of the Year Award in 1981. She dreaded the return to Stockton to accept the Arts Commission Award because the event promised to be much like a school reunion, with many of her teachers there, as well as several of the people she had written about. She recalls, "It was also a power thing to give me an event like that; there were various political enemies who wanted to confront one another. People with their own feuds showed up. It was the wild west, it was a Stockton event, and Stockton is where stories come from. So people from my books were there, plus people I didn't have time to write about."[30] In 1983 Kingston won the Hawaii Award for Literature. Later awards include the California Council for the Humanities Award (1985) and the California Governor's Award for the Arts (1989). In 1998 she was honored with the Fred Cody Lifetime Achievement Award from the Bay Area Book Reviewers Association.

In 1992 Kingston received a fellowship from the Lila Wallace Reader's Digest Fund and used the prize money to begin writing workshops for Vietnam veterans. She had the idea of holding such workshops much earlier, when she attended a retreat organized by Thich Nhát-Hanh, a Vietnamese Buddhist monk, called "Healing the Wounds of War." Veterans from America and Vietnam gathered for meditation and discussion, but it occurred to Kingston that the element of art was missing, so she incorporated a writing workshop during one day of the retreat. Later, when she won the fellowship from the Lila Wallace Reader's Digest Fund, she was asked to nominate a community project to work on; she decided to organize more workshops, to be held on a regular basis, and to open them to veterans of all wars.

Academic honors that have been bestowed upon Kingston include honorary doctoral degrees from Eastern Michigan University (1988), Colby College (1990), Brandeis University (1991), and the University of Massachusetts (1991). She was a Guggenheim fellow in 1981 and received the Brandeis University National Women's Committee Major Book Collection Award in 1990. National recognition of the extent of Kingston's contribution to American literature has taken the form of the 1990 Award in Literature from the American Academy and Institute of Arts and Letters. In 1992 she was inducted into the American Academy of Arts and Sciences and in September 1997 she was presented with a National Humanities Medal by President Bill Clinton.

NOTES

1. Karen Horton, "*Honolulu* Interview: Maxine Hong Kingston," in *Conversations with Maxine Hong Kingston,* edited by Paul Skenazy and Tera Martin (Jackson: University Press of Mississippi, 1998), p. 7.

2. Maxine Hong Kingston, *China Men* (New York: Knopf, 1980; reprint, New York: Vintage, 1989), p. 243. Subsequent page citations are given parenthetically in the text.

3. Timothy Pfaff, "Talk with Mrs. Kingston," in *Conversations with Maxine Hong Kingston,* p. 16.

4. Arturo Islas and Marilyn Yalom, "Interview with Maxine Hong Kingston," in *Conversations with Maxine Hong Kingston,* p. 28.

5. Kingston, *The Woman Warrior* (New York: Knopf, 1976; reprint, New York: Vintage, 1989), p. 48. Subsequent page citations are given parenthetically in the text.

6. Skenazy, "Coming Home," in *Conversations with Maxine Hong Kingston,* p. 115.

7. Kingston, *Hawai'i One Summer* (Honolulu: University of Hawaii Press, 1998), p. 12. Subsequent page citations are given parenthetically in the text.

8. Pfaff, "Talk with Mrs. Kingston," p. 17.

9. Kay Bonetti, "An Interview with Maxine Hong Kingston," in *Conversations with Maxine Hong Kingston,* p. 35.

10. Gary Kubota, "Maxine Hong Kingston: Something Comes from Outside Onto the Paper," in *Conversations with Maxine Hong Kingston,* p. 1.

11. Bonetti, "An Interview with Maxine Hong Kingston," p. 34.

12. Jody Hoy, "To Be Able to See the Tao," in *Conversations with Maxine Hong Kingston,* p. 62.

13. Islas and Yalom, "Interview with Maxine Hong Kingston," p. 26.

14. Pfaff, "Talk with Mrs. Kingston," p. 15.

15. Islas and Yalom, "Interview with Maxine Hong Kingston," p. 25.

16. Kubota, "Maxine Hong Kingston: Something Comes from Outside Onto the Paper," p. 3.

17. Ibid., p. 4.

18. Hoy, "To Be Able to See the Tao," p. 48.

19. Pfaff, "Talk with Mrs. Kingston," p. 20.

20. Ibid., p. 15.

21. Ibid., p. 14.

22. Ibid., p. 15.

23. Islas and Yalom, "Interview with Maxine Hong Kingston," p. 24.

24. Kubota, "Maxine Hong Kingston: Something Comes from Outside Onto the Paper," p. 3.

25. Bonetti, "An Interview with Maxine Hong Kingston," p. 35.

26. Hoy, "To Be Able to See the Tao," p. 49.

27. Ibid., p. 57.

28. Paula Rabinowitz, "Eccentric Memories: A Conversation with Maxine Hong Kingston," in *Conversations with Maxine Hong Kingston,* p. 69.

29. Charles Elliot, quoted in Horton, "*Honolulu* Interview: Maxine Hong Kingston," p. 6.

30. Hoy, "To Be Able to See the Tao," p. 65

KINGSTON AT WORK

GETTING ESTABLISHED

As a young girl Kingston developed the habit of writing down her thoughts and ideas. From these notes she developed her first two books, *The Woman Warrior* and *China Men*. Much of *The Woman Warrior* was written in Hawaii, though Kingston admits that she had been working on the book ever since she started writing as a child: "In a sense you could say that I was working on these books for 20 or 30 years, but in another sense I wrote them just a few years ago."[1] In contrast to the cramped conditions in which the young Kingston had to struggle to find the space to write, Hawaii offered an ideal working atmosphere. The tranquility of the islands allowed her the opportunity to think, and the Hawaiian landscapes heightened what she calls the sensory perceptions that are essential for her to write well. Kingston has said that while she does not write what she sees—these sensory perceptions are not used in such a simplistic way in her creative process—she does need the sense of being fully alive in order to realize her creativity.

This creative process is important because Kingston does not rely upon research to generate the materials for her writing. Research confirms details of the large historical movements of a particular period, or the style of clothes people wore then, but for Kingston these details are incidental to the really important aspect of her writing: the representation of feelings, emotions, or relations among people. As she has observed, "I feel that it [literary inspiration] comes from the heightened moments in all our lives when we are really aware of what it feels like to be a person or what life is all about. You don't feel it too often, but every once in a while you feel it. I want to put that feeling into writing or I want to write words so that when somebody reads it, they can have that feeling."[2] Her vision of what it means to be fully human, then, is what Kingston strives to represent in her writing.

Kingston at the time her 1980 book *China Men* was published

Kingston has two main methods of writing. One is seen in the genesis of the first poem she ever remembers writing, which came to her, she says, in a kind of trance; creating in this way, she is overcome suddenly with the knowledge of what she must write and the irresistible urge to write it down immediately: "I might be anywhere when it comes, and I could end up writing all over the floor or up the walls and not know what is going on. It is like having a fit."[3] The other method is much more controlled and self-conscious. Kingston deliberately writes as much as she can, according to what comes into her mind, and the process of writing induces a kind of visionary state. The writing she produces in this way often requires extensive revision and reworking, and it is in the process of revising that she can take conscious control of her materials and shape them with her literary artistry, giving the material a rational structure and grammatical form. The dominant images rather than the actual story come to Kingston first in the process of writing. So revision or reworking is a search for the correct expression that will connect with the visual images and make those images present to the reader. She then returns to the original material and rewrites it until she is satisfied with it.

HAWAII AS INSPIRATION

"Even our friends with Ph.D.s see things in Hawai'i. Our friend from Minnesota kept telling us about the row of fishermen walking in the ocean with torches at night. 'They're chanting to attract the fish,' he said. Later, he learned he was describing the march of the dead warriors. Another sensible friend tells us how he ran from block to block to dodge the nightwalkers. 'I would've died if they crossed my path,' he said. The most unimaginative people hear the hoof-beats of the princess's horse, and lock their doors. They wrestle with invisible foes at ceremonial grounds, see—and photograph—the face of the goddess Pele in the volcano fire, offer the old woman—Pele in disguise—water when she comes asking for it, floating on smoking feet."

Maxine Hong Kingston

From "Strange Sightings," in *Hawai'i One Summer* (Honolulu: University of Hawaii Press, 1998), p. 54.

Kingston worked on *The Woman Warrior* for more than two years before showing it to an agent. During that time she kept the manuscript to herself rather than showing parts of the work-in-progress to friends and colleagues. Aware of her limited knowledge of the literary market, she chose to approach an agent rather than go directly to any publishers. She guessed that an agent would know of small presses in the event that the larger publishers rejected her work. Kingston recalls, "I didn't realize that New York agents don't know the small presses. So when I found an agent, he looked immediately at the large presses and sold it almost right off."[4] Thus, she found publication quite easy to achieve. Despite her modest ambitions, she took the success of *The Woman Warrior* in stride. Only when *China Men* joined *The Woman Warrior* on the best-seller list at the same time was Kingston surprised. Although she had shared every new writer's dream of writing a best-seller, she had not thought it possible to have two simultaneous best-sellers.

John Leonard, reviewing *The Woman Warrior* in *The New York Times*, remarked, "Those rumbles you hear on the horizon are the big guns of autumn lining up, the howitzers of Vonnegut and Updike and Cheever and Mailer, the books that will be making loud noises for the next several months. But listen: this week a remarkable book has been quietly published; it is one of the best I've read for years."[5] Leonard detected a sea change in American literature signaled by the publication of Kingston's extraordinary first book.

The Woman Warrior met with extraordinary academic and popular acclaim, but Kingston's reaction to the success of her book was muted. She has explained her matter-of-fact acceptance of this acclaim as a consequence of her age. If she had been younger when she was suddenly catapulted into the spotlight, perhaps she might have been more deeply affected by the sudden fame. But at the age of thirty-eight, Kingston's private life was not greatly changed, except that she was compelled to acquire an unlisted telephone number. She was inundated with calls from people who had read her work and were sufficiently moved by it to contact her. These also included some unstable people as well as those who simply wished her well. Another change was the Kingstons' purchase of their first home. In *Hawai'i One Summer* Kingston included a piece titled "Our First House," in which she describes the change from being "renters," with all the freedom to move quickly and easily that that entails, to becoming householders, "one incarnation away from snail or turtle or kangaroo" (3). She writes proudly that she had never become a "housewife," someone who keeps house, but what drew her to this particular house was "a writer's garret, the very writer's garret of your imagination, bookshelves along an entire wall and a window overlooking plumeria in bloom and the ponds. If I could see through the foliage, I could look downhill and see the (restored) hut where Robert Louis Stevenson wrote his Hawai'i works" (4).

TECHNIQUES

The inspiration for Kingston's innovative narrative technique is her commitment to the idea that only the transformation of human consciousness can lead to changes in the way people live their lives. As she has put it, "the first step is to have that kind of consciousness that can create the world and save it. We have to change human consciousness and that's a step towards changing the material world."[6] This is why the say, "what silliness have you been up to now?" "That's a Ho

Chi Kuei for you," they say, no matter what we've done. It

was *more* complicated (and therefore worse) than "dog," which they

say affectionately, mostly to boys, they use "pig" and "stink

pig" *for* on girls, and only in an angry voice. The river-pirate

great-uncle called even my middle brother Ho Chi Kuei, and

he seemed to like him best. The maggot third great-uncle *even*

shouted, "Ho Chi Kuei!" even at the boy. I don't know any

Chinese I can ask without getting myself scolded or teased, so

I've been looking in books. So far I have the following

translations for "ho" and/or "chi": "centipede," "grub,"

"bastard carp," "chirping insect," "jujube tree," "pied wag-

tail," "grain sieve," "casket sacrifice," "water lily,"

"good frying," "non-eater," "dustpan -and-broom" *(but that's*

last is a synonym for "wife"). Or perhaps I've mis-romanized, *romanized*

the spelling wrong and it is "Hao Chi Kuei," which could mean they *are calling us* call us Good

Foundation Ghosts, the emigrants could be saying *that* we were born

on Gold Mountain and have advantages. Sometimes they scorn *us*

for having had it so easy how easy we have it, and sometimes they're delighted. They

also call us "Chu Sing," which means *or* bamboo node. They call

us Bamboo Nodes. Bamboo nodes obstruct water.

And Here in Hawaii, the Chinese from California are called

"katonks" because when the locals knock them/us down, their/our

- **288**

Typescript page from an early draft of *The Woman Warrior*

re-creation of a sense of vitality and the imagery to express that perception are essential to Kingston's writing. But the literary forms she inherited were designed primarily to express existing states of consciousness rather than to transform them. If she was to articulate new ways of being, then she had to invent a new literary language and form that would allow her to express these new states of consciousness.

One of the most characteristic elements of Kingston's style is her blending of the real and the fantastic or fictitious. For example, in the selection from *The Woman Warrior* titled "At the Western Palace," she recounts in detail the confrontation of her mother's sister, Moon Orchid, with the husband from whom she has been estranged for many years. Kingston quotes the dialogue that was spoken during the encounter; she describes in detail all the circumstances of the meeting. But at the beginning of the next piece, "A Song for a Barbarian Reed Pipe," she reveals that in fact the story has come to her at third hand, from one of her sisters, who heard it from the brother who drove his aunt to this meeting with her estranged husband but did not stay to witness the entire encounter. Kingston thus confuses the real and the fictitious in this episode. This "convoluted style,"[7] which is characteristic of *The Woman Warrior,* is something Kingston has claimed she strives to achieve because, in her view, life does not conform to the structure of a simple, linear narrative with a clearly defined beginning, middle, and end. Rather, life is confused and convoluted, and nothing is explained by an all-knowing narrator; thus, a book that accurately represents life is difficult to read and requires a great deal of work on the part of the reader. In *China Men,* however, Kingston simplified her narrative style and rose to a challenge she set herself—to use sentences that were simple and clear, yet communicated a complicated message. In *Tripmaster Monkey* Kingston returned to the "convoluted style" of *The Woman Warrior,* but she used a third-person narrator, Kuan Yin, the goddess of mercy, who comments upon the characters and the action. The narrative voice of *Tripmaster Monkey* thus controls and simplifies the significance of the narrative as it progresses.

Much of the ambiguity that characterizes Kingston's style arises from the tension between oral storytelling and written narrative. In the oral tradition, stories change with every telling, in response to the occasion and the needs of the teller and the listeners. Written stories are, by comparison, static and unchanging. Kingston inserts some of the dynamism of oral storytelling into her narratives by using ambiguity, so that the interpretation of the stories, if not the stories themselves, can change over time. In *The Woman Warrior,* for example, as she narrates the story of the No Name Aunt, who may be a victim of rape, seduction, or her own romantic ideals, Kingston refuses to specify what is the motivation of this character and with whom the blame ultimately lies for her fate.

The narrative structure of *The Woman Warrior* is that of a feminist *kunstlerroman* (artist novel). A *kunstlerroman* tells the story of an artist's development from childhood through maturity and concludes with the subject's mature realization that he or she is an artist. Traditionally, the *kunstlerroman* has told the story of a man's realization of his artistic destiny; the feminist *kunstlerroman* must therefore be a hybrid form that is modified to express a maturing feminine consciousness. The narrative must also accommodate some consideration of the special difficulties women confront when entering a traditionally male-dominated domain such as art or literature. *The Woman Warrior* is indeed such a hybrid form, comprised of autobiography, biography, myth, legend, and historical reconstruction.

In each of the five sections of *The Woman Warrior* a character or public mask (daughter, student, warrior, or writer) is explored who offers the narrator a model of femininity. But this multiplicity of roles, the fact that there are so many versions of femininity, renders identity itself mysterious. The form of the narrative seeks to articulate the conflicting forces that have shaped Kingston's identity. The disjunctions between China and America, the past and present, the mythic and the mundane, and the real and the recollected have been formative influences upon her. Kingston tries to find a voice with which to express her relationship with her mother and in this way reach an understanding of how women can relate to each other. Relations between women are complicated in the brutally misogynistic Chinese culture that her mother describes and the conflicting American culture within which Kingston lives. Consequently, the narrative voice is complicated and confusing—varying from subjective reconstruction (in the story of the No Name Aunt), imaginative construction (in Moon Orchid's story), or historical verisimilitude (in Kingston's representation of her mother in "Shaman"). Through the fragmentation of form—by shifting between first- and third-person narration—Kingston attempts to overcome the doubleness of her cultural heritage by creating an illusion of simultaneity within the reader's consciousness.

The narrative structure of *China Men* is similarly a hybrid form, made up of autobiography, myth, fantasy, and historical fact. Each chapter juxtaposes the life stories of Kingston's ancestors and of Kingston herself with parables that represent in a more compact fashion the significance of the story. The distinction between fact and fiction is not always clear, and in trying to navigate this ambiguous area, readers expe-

73

because it showed a willingness to work. But this week, they like "yes job"
and "yes money" because you wouldn't be taking jobs away from white workers."
The men groaned, "Some help." Those workers were ~~intent priceless,~~
~~bringing news, telling~~ which immigrant demons could be bribed and for
how much, telling what a relative ahead said so that the brother or uncle
would ~~answer consistently, slipping them notes from them.~~ Put this
with former paragraph on food, put all together with mother section.

Living the legal father's life. ~~He was let out of the wooden house~~
~~once, he circled the yard as far as the fence, where there were guards in~~
~~uniform. A guard threw him a ball and said,~~ motioning, "Play ball. Go
ahead. Play with it," as if they were a boy and could play. Even the
boys ~~didn't~~ play. "Who can be that lighthearted?" A couple of men did
throw the ball back and forth; nothing else to do. "We'd better start
~~learning American customs,~~" they said. "Leave out?

Jesus Demons entered the barracks and ~~sat right on the beds~~ to pester
them. They had white faces but Chinese words came out of their mouths.
They talked about how they were old China hands and how much they respected
Chinese. "I am not Chinese, I am a Gold Mountain man," ~~the man said,~~
the legal father heard, impressing him very much. However, a few
listened to them; the women listened to them, the women nodding as they
~~liked~~ women believed anything. "Would help us land if we converted?"
the men asked the Jesus Demons, who did not give a clear yes, so only
fools converted. At least in China, converts got a western eduction,
free clothes, food, a job, a place to live, a free burial. These
Island missionaries left ~~grisly~~ cards with pictures of a demon nailed
to a cross, probably a warning about what happened to you if you didn't
convert. Chinese crucified people too; they were not nailed like this
but tied to the wood and garroted. In China, there were
pictures of soldiers eating ~~the meat of~~ Christians; it looked like drumsticks
tattooed "meat."

The horror of these kinds of death added to the fear that was ~~already~~
in the Wooden House.

Everyday men were called out one by one at various intervals. The
legal father kept himself looking presentable, kempt. ~~one of those~~
~~the ~~ so they could,

rience Kingston's own halting attempts at cross-cultural understanding. Some guidance is given in the alternation of first- and third-person narrators: the latter are used for the historical and legendary stories, the former for autobiographical elements of the narrative.

In both *The Woman Warrior* and *China Men* Kingston used material that either actually happened or was a part of the Chinese American culture in which she grew up. She had no need for invention in these early works, and she has described the materials she used in the two books as gifts bestowed upon her by the circumstances of her birth and upbringing. Only with *Tripmaster Monkey* did she begin to invent a fictional world and to make up characters and incidents.

Kingston's use of myth has been criticized for lacking accuracy and not being faithful to the classical versions of Chinese legends. Instead of using the classical tales of high Chinese culture, she draws on what she calls the "small tradition" of Chinese popular culture, the tradition of poor, working-class people.[8] This mythology, and the versions of the stories Kingston uses, is specific not only to a class but also to the region in southern China from which her parents originally came. She uses these myths not simply to add an exotic texture to her writing or even to keep the stories current by retelling them. Rather, she believes that the myths of the past, while they may have a profound effect upon how life is experienced and interpreted, cannot be allowed to prescribe the future. Kingston employs traditional tales in combination with modern stories in order to represent the ways in which her characters must come to terms with the relationship between their inherited ideas and their actual, lived experiences. Simply to record a myth is, she claims, "just more ancestor worship. The way I keep the old Chinese myths alive is by telling them in a new American way."[9]

Kingston strenuously avoids treating the past in a sentimental way and instead addresses the more difficult question of what it means to be living in the present. For example, the story of the woman warrior who has the grievances of her village carved into her back was originally the story of a man, Yüch Fei, who has a vow carved into his back by his mother. Kingston took the story and transformed it into a woman's story; she has described how she "gave a man's myth to a woman, because it's part of the feminist war that's going on in *The Woman Warrior,* to take the men's stories away from them and give the strength of that story to a woman."[10]

The juxtaposition of myth and historical episodes in *China Men* serves the purpose of questioning not so much the truth as the usefulness of inherited myths and the values they represent. So the story "The Brother in Vietnam" is preceded by a mythic tale about a pacifist. Kingston raises questions through this implied contrast and comparison: "what good is it to go to Vietnam with that myth hanging in back of you? Does it help this person survive in Vietnam? Does it help him not to fight, or what?"[11] These questions are implied by the placement of the myth within the structure of the narrative; through such juxtapositions Kingston raises moral issues without explicitly stating the relation between inherited myths and the historical present. Her refusal to state how she is using the myths has led some critics to overlook her real interest, which is how the myths relate to contemporary life in America.

Kingston does not limit herself to the use of only Chinese myths and stories; she uses western stories as well, when they suit her purpose. For example, "The Adventures of Lo Bun Sun" in *China Men* is a version of the Robinson Crusoe story: Lo Bun Sun undergoes the immigrant experience of isolation, loneliness, danger, troubles, and survival.

In *Tripmaster Monkey* the protagonist, Wittman Ah Sing, does not have the support offered by the mythic stories in Kingston's earlier books. He is a fictional character based on the Monkey King of Chinese myth. Thus, the mythology provides a model for his character rather than a context within which his experiences can be interpreted. Other characters in the novel adopt mythic personae; that is, they act out the roles of various mythic characters. In the chapter titled "The Winners of the Party," Wittman assigns roles to his friends that they must act out. Wittman is Gwan Goong, Charley is Chang Fei, and Lance is Liu Pei; at one stage Lance breaks with his character and Wittman scolds him: "You have to be realistic."[12]

In *Tripmaster Monkey* the narrative voice is subtly different from that in Kingston's first two books, although she uses a feminine narrator in all three works, even when she is telling men's stories. She explains the difference between *The Woman Warrior* and *China Men* in terms of the narrative voice she adopted for each: "In a way, *The Woman Warrior* was a selfish book. I was always imposing my viewpoint on the stories. In *China Men* the person who 'talks-story' is not so intrusive. I bring myself in and out of the stories, but in effect, I'm more distant. The more I was able to understand my characters, the more I was able to write from their point of view and the less interested I was in relating how I felt about them."[13] Kingston is even more "distant" from the characters of *Tripmaster Monkey,* in which she uses an omniscient narrator. This kind of narrative voice has been routinely thought of as masculine because at the time when the novel was reaching its characteristic form, in the nineteenth chinamen. The Rock Springs Massacre began in a large coal mine owned by the Union Pacific; the outnumbered chinamen were shot in the back as they ran to Chinatown, which the demons burned. They shot chinamen forced out into the open; demon women and children threw the wounded back in the flames. (There was a rumor of a good white lady in Green Springs who hid China Men in the Pacific Hotel and shamed the demons away.) The hunt went on for a month before federal troops came. The count of the dead was inexact because bodies were mutilated and pieces scattered all over the Wyoming Territory. No white miners were indicted, but the government gave $150,00 in reparations to victims' families. There were many family men, then there were settlers. Ah Goong was running elsewhere during the Driving Out of Tacoma, Seattle, Oregon City, Albania, and Marysville. The entire chinamen population of Tacoma was packed into boxcars and sent to Portland, where they were run out of town. China Men returned to Seattle, though, and refused to sell their land and stores but fought until the army came; the demon rioters were tried and acquitted. And when the Boston police imprisoned and beat 234 chinamen, it was 1902, and Ah Goong had already reached San Francisco or China, and perhaps San Francisco again.

In Second City (Sacramento), he spent some of his railroad money at the theater. The main actor's face was painted red with thick black eyebrows and long black beard, and when he strode onto the stage, Ah Goong recognized the hero, Guan Goong; his puppet horse had red nostrils and rolling eyes. Ah Goong's heart leapt to recognize hero and horse in the wilds of America. Guan Goong murdered his enemy—crash! bang! of cymbals and drum—and left his home village—sad, sad flute music. But to the glad clamor of cymbals entered the friends—Liu Pei (pronounced the same as Running Nose) and Chang Fei. In a joyful burst of pink flowers, the three men swore the Peach Garden Oath. Each friend friend sang an aria to friendship; together they would fight side by side and live and die one for all and all for one. Ah Goong felt as warm as if he were with friends at a party. Then Guan Goong's archenemy, the sly Ts'ao Ts'ao, captured him and two of Liu Pei's wives, the Lady Kan and the Lady Mi. Though Ah Goong knew they were boy actors, he basked in the presence of Chinese ladies. They traveled to the capital, the soldiers waving horsehair whisks, signifying horses, the ladies walking between horizontal banners, signifying palanquins. All the prisoners were put in one bedroom, but Guan Goong stood all night outside the door with a lighted candle in his hand, singing an aria about faithfulness. When the capital was attacked by a common enemy, Guan Goong fought the biggest man in one-to-one combat, a twirling, jumping sword dance that strengthened the China Men who watched it. Guan Goong's two partners heard about the feats of the man with the red face and intelligent horse. The three friends were reunited and fought until Liu Pei secured his rightful kingdom.

Ah Goong felt refreshed and inspired. He called out Bravo like the demons in the audience, who had not seen theater before. Guan

Galley proof from *China Men* with Kingston's revisions

century, the main practitioners of the genre were men. In addition, in Kingston's view, "the nineteenth-century novel was written at a time when we believed in a white, male God." Her achievement lies in her creation of an omniscient narrator who is an ethnic woman rather than a white male, as she explains: "I think of my narrator now as Kuan Yin [goddess of mercy]. This is a big change—a narrator who people can see right away is a woman. She is always helping the woman characters out in there [*sic*], giving Wittman a bad time."[14] Though the narrator does comment upon Wittman and the things he does, often dismissively by calling him "poor monkey" (21) and the like, the narrative is focused through the consciousness of Wittman. The narrator knows Wittman's thoughts, feelings, motivations, history, and hopes for the future; all of the other characters are represented as they affect Wittman and his progress through the narrative.

One of the aspects of Kingston's writing that is often overlooked by critics is the humor of her work. She speculates that perhaps most readers are afraid to laugh at the humor of ethnic writing but notes that members of her own family, such as her brothers and sisters, find her work quite funny. She reasons that "when people come to ethnic writing they have such reverence for it or are so scared that they don't want to laugh."[15] Kingston uses various kinds of humor. She makes puns, such as the narrator's joking comment in *Tripmaster Monkey* that Wittman feels "agoraphobic on Market Street" (67), which plays on the Greek word for the space or plaza in the middle of a town and also the Latin root of the English word *agriculture*. She also uses literary allusions for comic effect: Wittman refers to Hermann Hesse's novel *Steppenwolf* (1927), which tells of a quest for mystical enlightenment that offers a parallel with his own quest. But in an episode in which he attempts to set up a display of children's bicycles and gets his tie caught in a bicycle chain, Kingston uses the allusion in a comic, literal sense: "he cut the tie with the dull scissors on a string tied to the counter. The Steppenwolf gnaws his leg free from the trap of steel, he thought" (54).

Kingston also employs a more raucous form of humor that is quite deliberate. She explains, "Chinese and Chinese Americans are the most raucous people: they laugh so much, they're telling jokes, and they're always standing up and performing for one another. They're *so* outgoing. . . . I also think that being able to laugh and to be funny—those are really important *human* characteristics, and when we say that people don't have those characteristics, then we deny them their humanity."[16] Examples of this kind of humor are represented by Mrs. Chang, an elderly woman Wittman meets while registering as unemployed, who thanks him for his help by telling him the story of how war on earth was started by a fart. In *China Men* Bak Goong, the Hawaiian grandfather, tells jokes to make fun of the Christian missionaries who cannot understand what he is saying and to make his work on a sugar plantation easier to bear.

Vivid imagery dominates the stories Kingston tells. Perhaps the most dominant image in *The Woman Warrior* is that of ghosts. In the context of the book, ghosts are those who threaten Chinese traditions by drawing people away from Chinese culture or by subverting it, as the No Name Aunt does. These threats to traditional culture are rendered void and deprived of reality when they are thought of as ghosts. Most terrifying to the young Kingston were the ghosts of the dead and tortured Chinese people that her mother conjured up in her stories. In *China Men* Anglo-American society is the world of ghosts, a world more like that represented in myths and tales than historical reality. Ghosts represent aspects of the loss of ethnicity—for example, Sao is haunted by the ghost of the dead mother he has abandoned in favor of his life in America. In "The Ghostmate" a ghost-woman, perhaps symbolizing American women, mystifies a young wanderer from China and keeps him from returning to his wife and children. Anglo colonialists are referred to as demons by Bak Goong as he works in the sugarcane fields of Hawaii; this reference provides a context for later uses of the terms "white demon" or "white devil" in the narrative.

The stories or "talk-story" that Kingston repeats in her narratives perform several roles. In *The Woman Warrior* talk-story can sustain superstitions or embody warnings, and stories can also offer the chance to imagine unrealized possibilities. The No Name Aunt's story does all of these things. Telling can be a form of vengeance. The entire text of *The Woman Warrior* is a discontinuous talk-story relating how Kingston developed as an artist and a woman. The narrative concludes with her mature realization: "Be careful what you say. It comes true. It comes true. I had to leave home in order to see the world logically, logic the new way of seeing. . . . Shine floodlights into dark corners: no ghosts" (182). At the end she is able to express a new view of herself as a translator or mediator between cultures.

In *China Men* the Gold Mountain represents America, but from a mythical perspective. This concept frames the narrative—it is the subject of the first and last parables. The journey toward this promised land and the reality of life there is the point of the narrative. The image provides a significant analogy to the dominant Anglo image of America as the promised land of opportunity. The meanings of the image are multiple: riches and escape from poverty, but also hardship, discrimination, and separation from family. Life in America often means forgetting the past for characters such as Sao, who is annoyed by the letters his mother in China sends him before she dies of starvation. Even Kingston's father, according to her, can "only look and talk Chinese" and provides her with "No stories. No past" (14). Alternatively, the image can mean an obsessive desire to return to China, as it does for Uncle Bun, the madman and communist, or Bak Goong, Maxine's great-grandfather.

In the first parable in *China Men* Tang Ao, upon reaching the Gold Mountain, finds himself violated and emasculated; this is the experience common to all the Chinamen whose journey to America Kingston describes. In the last parable the Gold Mountain is reduced to the image of a gold needle—a needle in the haystack—and the Chinamen who have sought their fortunes on the Gold Mountain have been sorely deceived. They have transformed the country into gold, making it rich by investing it with their labor, but they are permitted to live only on the margins of this wealth.

The twin concepts of silence and articulation are as important in *China Men* as they are in *The Woman Warrior:* Bak Goong overcomes the injunction to silence on the sugar plantation, and Kingston tries to understand her father's silences, just as in *The Woman Warrior* she struggles to overcome her own silence and find her voice. Language in her work crystallizes her cross-cultural experience. Early reviewers commented upon the exotic, oriental nature of Kingston's language; these comments prompted her to ask in exasperation why they were unable to hear her American slang.[17] Many of the stories in *The Woman Warrior* and *China Men* are told by Brave Orchid, but they are told to her daughter who, in turn, narrates them to the reader—in her own American idiom.

Kingston has described how the writing of her first two books was largely a matter of translation from Chinese into American language. The inspiration for *Tripmaster Monkey,* however, came primarily from the language of the 1960s, the time in which the novel is set: "I love that language of the Sixties, the slang of the Sixties. And all those words that were invented to describe psychedelic states, visions, . . . Zen gestures, pacifist activities, like sit-ins, and be-ins, and love-ins. All those words that were made up, 'Flower Power,' and all that."[18]

REVISION

The main problem Kingston faces as a writer, she confesses, is finding the discipline to sit down and write. She admits that writing is a difficult and painful activity, and that it is easy to find distractions: "Writing is a very painful act. I try to start writing in the mornings, but I fool around and put it off to wash dishes or sharpen my pencils. I'm pretty regular on writing every day, but sometimes I start late and end up finishing in the afternoons."[19] She also admits that working to support herself has created an obstacle to writing, a reference to the high-school teaching in which she was engaged while writing *The Woman Warrior*. While at work on *China Men* she was a visiting professor of English at the University of Hawaii in Honolulu, and she continued to teach while writing *Tripmaster Monkey*. Throughout this time, she wrote every day out of habit, even when she found it difficult to make herself sit down to write. She looks to the positive side of even these difficult periods, remarking that "some days when it's really bad, it's good for you, too. As long as you feel it's bad, you keep working on it. And you feel it's bad because you have a kind of vision of what it should be and so you strive and work and re-work. But when you feel good, maybe it's very deceptive, because then you don't re-work."[20]

KINGSTON ON THE CREATIVE PROCESS

"I keep some Lew Welch advice over my desk: 'When I write, my only concern is accuracy. I try to write accurately from the poise of mind which lets us see that things are exactly what they seem. I never worry about beauty, if it is accurate there is always beauty. I never worry about form, if it is accurate there is always form.' I ditto this for my students at the beginnings of courses, and tell them I have not much more to teach them, but they don't believe me, and stay."

Maxine Hong Kingston

From "Lew Welch: An Appreciation," *Hawai'i One Summer* (Honolulu: University of Hawaii Press, 1998), p. 65.

Kingston revises her work extensively before the final version is ready for publication. For example, *Tripmaster Monkey* was a thousand pages long at one stage, and she was afraid that the book would never be finished. She spent months revising *China Men* (then tentatively called "The Gold Mountain Heroes") shut away in an apartment in New York while her husband auditioned for stage plays. The book went through at least eight drafts, and her revision of the galley proofs was so extensive that the book had to be reset to accommodate all the changes. Her editor, Charles Elliott, has remarked that Kingston's work requires little additional editing once he receives it, but he does have some difficulty wresting the manuscript out of her hands.

The image of writing that is represented in Kingston's works is quite ambivalent. The ability of writers to effect the resolution of conflicts or to transform the world is limited. She remarks, "the frustration I feel is that writers have the power to change the world only a little bit at a time. We conquer a reader at a time. We change the atmosphere of the world, and we change moods here and there, whereas the people who have the guns and the bombs have so much direct power."[21]

CRITICAL RECEPTION

The initial response of Kingston's readers was quite positive; *The Woman Warrior* met with enthusiastic praise, especially from reviewers. The book was seen as representing a major innovation in contemporary American literature. Kingston was lauded as a major feminist and Chinese American writer, and hailed as a leader in the flowering of ethnic writing that characterized American literature in the latter part of the twentieth century.

The reception of Kingston's work has not been uniformly positive, however. She has been criticized for working in the genre of nonfiction rather than the novel. Autobiography is considered by some minority critics to be a lesser form than fiction; as Kingston explains, "you are not using imagination, and you present yourself as an oddity, an anthropological specimen."[22] The criticism leveled at her, then, is for her perceived failure as an Asian American writer to produce work that will be received as positively as possible. But Kingston's response is that she could have published her first two books as fiction; it was an arbitrary decision on the part of her editor to present them as autobiography.

Loudest and most insistent among the voices dissenting from the enthusiastic reception of Kingston's work is the criticism of male Chinese American writers. This group of critics is led by the playwright Frank Chin, who has accused her of compromising her work in order to appeal to a white readership. Chin has compared her unfavorably to Pocahontas, suggesting that she has sold out her people in order to make herself popular with white readers. In his essay "The Most Popular Book in China" Chin includes a witty but savage parody of *The Woman Warrior,* which he titles "Unmanly Warrior." The parody is narrated by a French girl living in China who tells of her French ancestry. Chin uses the story of Joan of Arc in place of the legend of the woman warrior, Fa Mu Lan. He concludes by turning his attention explicitly to Kingston and the Chinese American playwright David Henry Hwang. Chin argues that Kingston and Hwang misrepresent Chinese legends and historical facts, but whereas the legend of Joan of Arc is "obscure and esoteric" to the French, the Chinese legends that are corrupted by Kingston are not obscure to the Chinese. He asks, "The violation of history and of fact and of Joan of Arc makes no difference to the pleasure and stimulation the Chinese get from *Unmanly Warrior,* so why should the falsification of history, the not making plans to do himself in, and no more willed these seppuku movies — no more conjured up that gun — as built this city. His cowboy boots, plain brown Wellingtons, hit its pavements hard. Anybody serious about killing himself goes off the Bridge. The wind or shock knocks you out before impact. Oh, long before impact. Two hundred and thirty-five people had taken the question "To be or not to be?" seriously to heart, and answered, "Not to be." They take the side of the Bridge that faces land. And the City. The last City. Feet first. Coit Tower giving you the finger all the way down. Wittman would face the sea. And the setting sun. Dive. But he was not going to do that. Strange. These gun pictures were what was left of his childhood ability to see galaxies. Such glass cosmospheres there had once been, and planets with creatures, their doings, their colors. None abiding. In the Chronicle, a husband and wife, past eighty, too old to live, shot each other with a weak gun, and had to go to a doctor to have the bullets prized out of their ears. And, in June, in Viet Nam, a Buddhist burned himself to death on purpose; his name was

Manuscript page from an early draft of *Tripmaster Monkey*

white racist stereotypes and slurs in Kingston's prose and Hwang's theater mean anything to the pleasure whites derive from reading and seeing their work?"[23] Chin is as critical of their readers as he is of Kingston and Hwang themselves. He criticizes the readers for being satisfied with the racist stereotypes with which they are presented, and he criticizes the writers for offering stereotypes that identify the Chinese with the causes of white "perversions and debilitating insecurities": "The popular stereotype of the Chinese in white publishing, white religion, Hollywood and TV is a sickening pastiche of white perversions and socially unacceptable fantasies made speakable by calling them Chinese. Kingston and Hwang confirm the white fantasy that everything sick and sickening about the white self-image is really Chinese. That is their service to white ego."[24]

Kingston claims that Chin has not only criticized her work but has also personally threatened her. Some reviewers of *Tripmaster Monkey* suggested that the book is her way of seeking revenge on him and her other Chinese American male critics by creating an unpleasant character who resembles Chin in significant ways: both Wittman and Chin graduated from Berkeley in the early 1960s, come from Oakland, and are playwrights. Kingston disputes this identification, pointing out that, on the contrary, she sees the novel as "a kind of big love letter. If it is answering—if it is—then it's like he's sending me hate mail, and I send him love letters, it's like that. . . . [The novel] is not a *roman à clef* and I'm not trying to capture Frank or his language."[25]

Kingston's response to criticism such as Chin's was at first to attempt to engage in a dialogue with her critics. Later, she simply ignored them, pointing out that these critics, especially the Chinese American males, were using her work to further their own political aims. In particular, Kingston believes that her work does not bear out the claim that she somehow worked with or conspired with white American publishers to exclude Chinese American men from literary prominence. She explains, "Some people have said that the white male press or publishing industry will publish women, but they'll castrate male writers, and they say that this is why we don't have a major male novelist among Asian Americans."[26] While Kingston acknowledges that minority men have been treated badly by prejudice and racial discrimination, she also argues that their resentment is misplaced when it is directed at minority women. Kingston draws a parallel between Chin's attacks on her and the African American writer Ishmael Reed's attack on Alice Walker's representation of African American men in *The Color Purple* (1982). Kingston speculates, "Maybe what they say is exactly what's going on: the novel has been castrated out of them and all that's left is tremendous anger at women."[27]

Kingston expresses a surprising lack of concern about the reception of her work and little anxiety over whether her writing finds its way into print. Indeed, she has said that she long ago gave up worrying whether her work would be published. Kingston describes herself as writing from obsession. Writing is for her as much a part of everyday life as anything else she does from habit: "I have to eat, I have to breathe, I have to write . . . there's no question of stopping."[28]

NOTES

1. Arturo Islas and Marilyn Yalom, "Interview with Maxine Hong Kingston," in *Conversations with Maxine Hong Kingston,* edited by Paul Skenazy and Tera Martin (Jackson: University Press of Mississippi, 1998), p. 23.

2. Karen Horton, "*Honolulu* Interview: Maxine Hong Kingston," in *Conversations with Maxine Hong Kingston,* p. 12.

3. Timothy Pfaff, "Talk with Mrs. Kingston," in *Conversations with Maxine Hong Kingston,* p. 19.

4. Islas and Yalom, "Interview with Maxine Hong Kingston," p. 23.

5. John Leonard, "In Defiance of Two Worlds," *New York Times,* 17 September 1976, sec. 3, p. 21.

6. Shelley Fisher Fishkin, "Interview with Maxine Hong Kingston," in *Conversations with Maxine Hong Kingston,* p. 160.

7. Horton, "Honolulu Interview: Maxine Hong Kingston," p. 11.

8. Islas and Yalom, "Interview with Maxine Hong Kingston," p. 27.

9. Pfaff, "Talk with Mrs. Kingston," p. 18.

10. Kay Bonetti, "An Interview with Maxine Hong Kingston," in *Conversations with Maxine Hong Kingston,* p. 40.

11. Ibid., p. 41.

12. Maxine Hong Kingston, *Tripmaster Monkey: His Fake Book* (New York: Knopf, 1989), p. 142. Subsequent page citations are given parenthetically in the text.

13. Pfaff, "Talk with Mrs. Kingston," p. 18.

14. William Satake Blauvelt, "Talking with the Woman Warrior," in *Conversations with Maxine Hong Kingston,* p. 82.

15. Islas and Yalom, "Interview with Maxine Hong Kingston," p. 23.

16. Fishkin, "Interview with Maxine Hong Kingston," p. 164.

17. Kingston, "Cultural Mis-Reading by American Reviewers," in *Asian and Western Writers in Dialogue: New Cultural Identities,* edited by Guy Amirthanayagam (London: Macmillan, 1982), p. 58.

18. Marilyn Chin, "Writing the Other: A Conversation with Maxine Hong Kingston," in *Conversations with Maxine Hong Kingston,* p. 100.

19. Gary Kubota, "Maxine Hong Kingston: Something Comes from Outside Onto the Paper," in *Conversations with Maxine Hong Kingston,* p. 3.

20. Horton, "*Honolulu* Interview: Maxine Hong Kingston," p. 12.

21. Bonetti, "An Interview with Maxine Hong Kingston," p. 37.

22. Paula Rabinowitz, "Eccentric Memories: A Conversation with Maxine Hong Kingston," in *Conversations with Maxine Hong Kingston,* p. 75.

23. Frank Chin, "The Most Popular Book in China," in *Maxine Hong Kingston's The Woman Warrior: A Casebook,* edited by Sau-ling Cynthia Wong (New York & Oxford: Oxford University Press, 1999), p. 27.

24. Ibid., p. 28.

25. Blauvelt, "Talking with the Woman Warrior," p. 80.

26. Islas and Yalom, "Interview with Maxine Hong Kingston," p. 24.

27. Rabinowitz, "Eccentric Memories: A Conversation with Maxine Hong Kingston," p. 73.

28. Horton, "*Honolulu* Interview: Maxine Hong Kingston," p. 12.

KINGSTON'S ERA

INTRODUCTION

Kingston's writing has been heavily influenced by her cultural, social, and political milieu. The historical experience of Chinese immigrants in America provided much of the material for her first two books, *The Woman Warrior* and *China Men*. Kingston's work has also been shaped by her feminist awareness. When *The Woman Warrior* was published in 1976, the women's liberation movement was forcing substantial changes in the position of women in America. These changes were largely legislative, based upon the principles of equal opportunity and affirmative action, but the raising of women's consciousness and making women more aware of the nature of their oppression produced material changes in the daily lives of many American women. Kingston attended the University of California, Berkeley, from 1958 to 1962, returning to study for a teaching certificate from 1964 to 1965; during these years the campus was a hotbed of student unrest and political protest. The Civil Rights movement, which had emerged as a force in American politics in the 1950s, together with popular opposition to the Vietnam War and the conscription of American men to fight in that conflict, produced a student protest movement in which Kingston was actively involved. The protest against war is represented in her writing in the theme of pacifism, which is twinned with the theme of conflict. She asks how it is possible to resolve conflict peaceably yet effectively, and how it is possible to return home from a war and live a normal life. The idea of the writing workshops that Kingston organized for war veterans was motivated by her concern that the trauma of war be transmuted into art and thus lead to healing. Not only in her fiction but also in her continuing work with veterans of all wars, Kingston has made the experience of war a central focus of her literary career.

MODERN CHINESE HISTORY

Kingston's work focuses on the experience of Chinese immigrants in America, and she assumes the reader has some knowledge of

Kingston in 1982 at her home in Manoa Valley, Honolulu

Chinese history to provide a context for the myths, legends, and histories she uses in her representation of immigrant culture. Before the nineteenth century, Chinese contact with Europe was restricted to the port of Canton (Guangzhou), and contact between Chinese and foreigners was strictly limited. From the mid nineteenth century, China increased its contact with Europe. In 1842 the Treaty of Nanking brought an end to the Opium War, which had been sparked by the Chinese seizure of chests of opium that were being smuggled into China by British merchants. The treaty gave Hong Kong to Great Britain and opened five Chinese ports to British residence and trade. Between 1850 and 1864 millions of Chinese died in the civil war known as the Taiping Rebellion. The participants in the rebellion belonged to a quasi-religious group that combined Christian with traditional Chinese beliefs. Their influence threatened the position of both the Ch'ing Dynasty and their philosophy of Confucianism. Foreign powers assisted the Ch'ing with some military aid in order to maintain the treaties that favored their trade with China. A war with Japan in 1894 to 1895 resulted in the significant weakening of China, with the recognition of Japan's control over Korea, Japan's annexation of Taiwan, and the granting of further trading rights and territory to France, Germany, Russia, and Great Britain.

The Chinese empire appeared to be crumbling, but the Chinese people expressed a desire to remain as one nation, and in 1899 the United States persuaded the European powers to accept an Open Door policy guaranteeing all nations the right to trade with China on an equal basis. The Chinese reaction against increasing Western and Christian influences led to the formation of secret societies dedicated to the fight against these influences. In the Boxer Rebellion of 1900 these societies organized a campaign of terror, attacking and killing Europeans and Christian Chinese. The rebellion was crushed by a force comprised of troops from six foreign nations. In its wake a program of government reform was established. This reform program ended the Confucian civil-service examinations (in *China Men* Kingston describes her father attending the very last of these examinations) and created a modern school system. A Western-style army was organized, the provinces were allowed to elect their own legislatures, and the central government promised to adopt a constitution.

The republican movement, led by Sun Yat-sen, gained force despite these reforms. In 1911 the Republic of China was created, but the former revolutionaries soon reorganized as the Kuomintang (national people's party) to oppose the corruption of the new president, Yüan Shih-k'ai. Yüan's attempts to reestablish the empire and to style himself emperor failed. With the Nationalists in exile in Japan, the real power in China lay with provincial warlords. In 1928 the Nationalists, led by Chiang Kai-shek, defeated the warlords and the Chinese Communists and united the nation under a single government. In 1931 the Japanese occupied Manchuria and extended their military influence in northern China, beginning the long conflict that culminated in the conflict in the Pacific between 1937 and 1945. China joined the Allies and entered World War II in December 1941. The country received aid from the Allies, but the war against Japan weakened the Nationalist government and allowed the Communists to gain in strength and influence. Mao Zedong led the Chinese Communists on their long march (1934–1935) to the Shensi (Shaanxi) province; by the end of the war the Communists controlled a large area of northern China.

The United States intervened in the conflict between the Nationalists and Communists in 1946 by sending an envoy to attempt to find a political settlement. This diplomatic mission failed, and full-scale civil war broke out. In 1949 the Communists defeated the Nationalists and established the People's Republic of China. The Nationalists were forced to the island of Taiwan. In 1953 China began its first Five-Year Plan for economic growth, and in 1958 the Communists launched the Great Leap Forward, the second Five-Year Plan, in an attempt to accelerate economic development. In fact, the Great Leap Forward retarded the country's development by creating economic depression and food shortages, which lasted until 1962. The Cultural Revolution of 1966 to 1969 was Mao's attempt to ensure that China remained a radical Communist state based on the principle of a classless society. During this movement universities were closed, many provincial governments were seized by radicals, and all aspects of life in China were disrupted.

In 1971 Henry Kissinger, then serving as head of the U.S. National Security Council, traveled secretly to Peking to explore the possibility of establishing diplomatic relations between the United States and China. That same year China was admitted to the United Nations when America dropped its opposition to Chinese membership, and in 1972 President Richard Nixon made an official visit to China. At the conclusion of his trip the American and Chinese governments issued the Shanghai Communiqué, which anticipated the establishment of normal diplomatic relations. In 1976, the year in which *The Woman Warrior* was published, Communist Party Chairman Mao and Premier Zhou Enlai died. When the power struggle that followed Mao's death had been resolved, Deng Xiaoping emerged as the country's strongest leader. Since this period when relations were first normalized between China and the United States, developments in Chinese politics and culture have been regular news items in America.

THE CHINESE IMMIGRANT EXPERIENCE

The history of the Chinese in the United States is one largely of prejudice and discrimination, but it is also an invisible history of which most Americans are not aware. Kingston seeks to expose the true history of Chinese immigration in her writing. The exposé of injustice is part of her attempt to seek revenge, through writing, for the damage inflicted upon the Chinese community and members of her family by racial prejudice. In *China Men* she describes the phenomenon that she calls "the Driving Out" (145). After the transcontinental railroad was completed, and while the officials posed for photographs, the Chinese who labored so heroically on the project began to disperse. "It was dangerous to stay" (145), Kingston comments. In the pages that follow she documents this danger by telling of the torture, lynching, and murder of the Chinese. She writes of her grandfather Ah Goong, who "slid down mountains, leapt across valleys and streams, crossed plains, hid sometimes with companions and often alone, and eluded bandits who would hold him up for his railroad pay and shoot him for practice as they shot Injuns and jackrabbits. . . . In China bandits did not normally kill people, the booty [was] the main thing, but here the demons killed for fun and hate" (146).

The chapter titled "The Laws," which is strategically located in the center of the narrative in *China Men*, lists in chronological order the legislation enacted by the United States and California that

THE COMMUNIST REVOLUTION IN CHINA

"The news from China has been confusing. It also had something to do with birds. I was nine years old when the letters made my parents, who are rocks, cry. My father screamed in his sleep. My mother wept and crumpled up the letters. She set fire to them page by page in the ashtray, but new letters came almost every day. The only letters they opened without fear were the ones with red borders, the holiday letters that mustn't carry bad news. The other letters said that my uncles were made to kneel on broken glass during their trials and had confessed to being landowners. They were all executed, and the aunt whose thumbs were twisted off drowned herself. Other aunts, mothers-in-law, and cousins disappeared; some suddenly began writing to us again from communes or Hong Kong. They kept asking for money."

Maxine Hong Kingston

From *The Woman Warrior: Memoirs of a Girlhood Among Ghosts* (New York: Knopf, 1976), p. 50.

restricted Chinese immigration to the United States. The chapter begins with a quotation from the Burlingame Treaty of 1868, which set out an agreement between the United States and the emperor of China to allow their citizens and subjects the right to migrate and emigrate "for the purposes of curiosity, of trade, or as permanent residents" (152). Kingston begins with this treaty because it establishes an ironic context for the list of anti-Chinese legislation that follows. The 1870 Nationality Act allowed only "free whites" and "African aliens" to apply for naturalization, thus excluding the Chinese (152–153). In 1878 the Californian Constitutional Convention created a constitution prohibiting Chinese from entering California and instituting a system of penalties for those who might transport them. Cities and counties were empowered to confine Chinese to designated areas or to banish them, and they were among those barred from attending public schools. Special taxes to be paid only by the Chinese were created, and they were prohibited from owning land. Employers could be fined for hiring Chinese workers, and Chinese could not testify against a white man in a court of law.

The Burlingame Treaty was modified in 1880 so that, in return for government protection against lynching, the immigration of Chinese laborers would be limited. In 1881 the treaty was suspended for a twenty-year period, although Chinese already resident in America by 1882 were allowed to stay; they could also leave and reenter the country with a Certificate of Return. In 1882 Congress passed the first Chinese Exclusion Act, banning the immigration of Chinese laborers for a ten-year period; only a few temporary visas were issued to Chinese merchants and scholars. The Exclusion Act was refined in 1884, with increased fines and harsher sentences. In 1888 the Scott Act declared Certificates of Return void, so that some twenty thousand Chinese formerly resident in the United States were stranded outside the country. The Scott Act also decreed that Certificates of Residence must be shown upon demand, on pain of deportation. The Geary Act of 1892 extended the 1882 Exclusion Act for ten more years and decreed that Chinese living illegally in the United States should serve one year of hard labor before deportation.

Chinese Americans sought to fight this discriminatory legislation in the courts, forming the Equal Rights League and the Native Sons of the Golden State for this purpose. But in 1904 the Chinese Exclusion Acts were extended indefinitely and made to apply to Hawaii and the Philippines in addition to the continental United States. The 1924 Immigration Act excluded Chinese women and decreed that any American who married a Chinese—woman or man—would lose his or her citizenship. This legislation complemented the antimiscegenation laws (laws against mixed-race marriages) adopted by many states. The law also placed limits on the number of immigrants from each ethnic group that would be permitted each year. The Chinese Exclusion Act of 1882 was repealed in 1943, but from 1882 to 1943 the act had restricted Chinese immigration to teachers, students, merchants, and diplomats.[1] Kingston remarks in *China Men* that in 1943 "Japanese invaders were killing Chinese civilians in vast numbers; it is estimated that 10 million died. Chinese immigration into the United States did not rise" (157). When Congress passed the War Bride Act in 1946, allowing European and Japanese wives of returning soldiers into the country, a separate provision was enacted under which the wives and children of Chinese Americans were required to apply for entry as "non-quota immigrants" (157). The Refugee Act of 1948 applied only to Europeans; under the Displaced Persons Act of the same year, ethnic Chinese living in the United States could apply for citizenship, but only through 1954.

MIGRATING SPIRITS

"According to mystical people, spiritual forces converge at Hawai'i, as do ocean currents and winds. Kahuna, keepers and teachers of the old religion and arts (such as song writing, the hula, navigation, taro growing), still work here. The islands attract refugee lamas from Tibet, and the Dalai Lama and the Black Hat Lama have visited them. Some kahuna say they see tree spirits fly from branch to branch; the various winds and rains are spirits, too; sharks and rocks have spirits. If ancestors and immortals travel on supernatural errands between China and the Americas, they must rest here in transit, nothing but ocean for thousands of miles around. They landed more often in the old days, before the sandalwood trees were cut down."

Maxine Hong Kingston

From "Strange Sightings," in *Hawai'i One Summer* (Honolulu: University of Hawaii Press, 1998), p. 53.

After the Communist Revolution of 1949 Congress passed a series of acts for the relief of Chinese refugees, but at the same time, Chinese residents in the United States were deported as "subversives or anarchists," Kingston notes in *China Men* (158). After the Revolution, Chinese Americans were forbidden to send money to relatives in China. In 1965 the Immigration and Nationality Act altered the quota system by redefining national origin to refer to country of birth rather than race. Amendments to this act in 1968 replaced the concept of national origin with restrictions on the number of immigrants from each of the two hemispheres. A per-country quota remained for the Eastern Hemisphere, with no quota for the Western Hemisphere. This system was changed in 1976, when the per-country limit on immigration was extended to the Western Hemisphere. In 1978 a worldwide

RACIAL SLURS

"On drives along the windward side of O'ahu, I like looking out at the ocean and seeing the pointed island offshore, not much bigger than a couple of houses—Mokoli'i Island, but nobody calls it that. I had a shock when I heard it's called Chinaman's Hat. That's what it looks like, all right, a crown and brim on the water. I had never heard 'Chinaman' before except in derision when walking past racists and had had to decide whether to pretend I hadn't heard or to fight."

Maxine Hong Kingston

From "Chinaman's Hat," in *Hawai'i One Summer* (Honolulu: University of Hawaii Press, 1998), p. 29.

limitation on immigration to the United States replaced the separate quotas for the two hemispheres, with special quotas for Southeast Asian refugees.

Prejudicial legislation affected all Chinese, but discrimination was experienced especially powerfully by the Chinese women who suffered oppression from both mainstream American society and also from patriarchal Chinese culture. As a consequence, female immigration from China to the United States has been limited. Chinese custom required the women to stay behind at home while the men traveled to the "Gold Mountain" (America) in order to make their fortunes. In 1852 only seven of the 11,794 Chinese in California were women, though by the 1880s there was one woman for every twenty men. From 1924 to 1930 a law specifically forbade the immigration of Chinese women to America (including the wives of Chinese men born in America who went to China to marry). In the decade that followed revision of the act in 1930, an average of only sixty Chinese women per year entered the United States.[2] Only after 1946, when the Chinese wives and children of Chinese Americans were permitted to apply as nonquota immigrants, did the number of ethnic Chinese in the United States begin to approach that of 1882, before the first Exclusion Act. Not until 1952 could Chinese women immigrate on the same terms as Chinese men.

One of the most frequently cited reasons for excluding Chinese from immigration and permanent residence in the United States was the perception that they were unwilling to assimilate with American society. Kingston points to the irony of this accusation, given that for many years it was illegal for a Chinese person to apply for American citizenship. She notes in *China Men* that in 1893 the Supreme Court ruled that Congress could expel those who "continue to be aliens, having taken no steps toward becoming citizens, and incapable of becoming such under the naturalization laws" (155). The refusal to assimilate, the maintenance of an "alien" ethnic life-style—these accusations reflect the emergence of Chinese neighborhoods, or "Chinatowns."

People on the streets of San Francisco's Chinatown, circa 1895–1906.
Photographs by Arnold Genthe.

In Kingston's work the reality of a Chinese community is important, whether or not that community is represented by a specific geographical location. She points out that the famous Chinatown of San Francisco is quite different from that of Stockton, California, where she grew up. In Stockton there is no single geographically defined Chinatown; instead there is a tight-knit Chinese community, unified by common traditions, rituals, and memories. Kingston has expressed her disappointment that early reviewers of *The Woman Warrior* failed to note that the setting of the narrative is Stockton and not San Francisco. In her essay "Cultural Mis-readings by American Reviewers" she writes of *The Woman Warrior:* "the book itself says that the Chinese Americans in the San Joaquin Valley town, which is its setting, are probably very different from the city slickers in San Francisco. I describe a long drive *away from* San Francisco to the smaller valley town, which I do not name; I describe Steinbeck country. Yet, *New West,* which published an excerpt, prefaced it by twice calling it a San Francisco story—ironically, it was the very chapter about the San Joaquin valley."[3]

San Francisco's Chinatown has a material reality that readers can visualize, which Stockton's Chinatown does not share. Kingston is aware of this difference. She remarks, "The Chinatown in San Francisco is seeable. It's defined. We know pretty much what it is. It makes us think that that's what we look for when we look for Chinatown in Stockton. But the Chinatown in Stockton looks nothing like the Chinatown in San Francisco."[4] Kingston gave an account of the differences between San Francisco's and Stockton's Chinatowns in a 1978 essay, "San Francisco's Chinatown: A View of the Other Side of Arnold Genthe's Camera." (Genthe was a German-born photographer who documented life in San Francisco's Chinatown in the 1890s and 1910s.) In the essay she describes how "a trip from Stockton to San Francisco is a journey into foreign territory—urban, competitive, the people like Hong Kong city slickers, not at all like the people in the San Joaquin Valley, where villager is still neighborly to villager as in the Chinese countryside they remember, helping one another, 'not Chinese against Chinese like in the Big City.'"[5] The Chinese Americans of Stockton live more as their forbears did in China: everyone works, no matter how rich they might be; the language spoken is a peasant dialect; everyone is known; and gossip unifies the tight-knit community.

KINGSTON'S TIME IN HISTORY

Three key cultural movements define the historical context of Kingston's work: the struggle for civil rights, opposition to the Vietnam War and the draft, and the women's liberation movement. These were the political currents in which Kingston was personally involved during her time at the University of California, Berkeley, in the 1960s. Her commitment to these movements for cultural and social change materially influenced the subject of her writing and her experimentation in literary form, as she sought new ways of expressing these ideas.

The Civil Rights movement achieved limited success in racial desegregation and integration through nonviolent actions such as the Montgomery bus boycott of 1955–1956 and the Greensboro sit-in of 1960. Such actions involved black people deliberately violating racist laws and practices. In these cases, in Montgomery, Alabama, a black woman named Rosa Parks refused to give up her seat on a bus to a white man, and in Greensboro, North Carolina, four black college students sat at a "whites only" lunch counter and demanded service. Student activists in the sit-in movement formed the Student Nonviolent Coordinating Committee to work with the group formed earlier in Alabama by Martin Luther King Jr., the Southern Christian Leadership Conference. These activists faced beatings, tear gas, and even death in their resistance of unjust and racist laws. A massive demonstration in which two hundred thousand people of all races marched toward the Lincoln Memorial in Washington, D.C., in August 1963, was the single largest civil-rights demonstration in American history. In 1964 Congress passed the Civil-Rights Act, which prohibited racial discrimination in hotels, restaurants, and public accommodations; it also brought an end to the segregation of public schools. The following year, the Voting Rights Act guaranteed the right to vote, ended literacy tests and other devices that blocked the right to vote, and authorized federal examiners to register voters.

Racial tension reached a climax in the mid 1960s with riots in the black neighborhood of Watts in Los Angeles in 1965, in more than forty American cities in the summer of 1966, and in Newark and Detroit in 1967. These urban riots were sparked by the perception that the Civil Rights movement had bene-

Civil-rights demonstrator being attacked by a police dog in Birmingham, Alabama, 3 May 1963

fited rural southern blacks but that northern urban blacks were confronted with problems that nonviolent activism and legislation could not solve. These problems included segregated and overcrowded inner-city housing, chronic unemployment, poverty, and crime. A radical movement promoting a philosophy of racial separatism or "black power" emerged, led by Malcolm X, Stokeley Carmichael, Huey P. Newton, and Eldridge Cleaver. Other minority groups became active in the Civil Rights movement, including Hispanics, under the leadership of the labor leader Cesar Chavez, and Native Americans through AIM (the American Indian Movement), which adopted a "red power" philosophy.

In the early 1960s increasing numbers of college students were involved in the Civil Rights movement, in SNCC activities, and in nonviolent activism such as sit-ins. But as legislative action on civil rights was slow to come about and as criticism mounted concerning America's increasing involvement in the conflict in Vietnam, young people became disillusioned not just with the structure of political life but with the values of American life in general. The student protest movement gained momentum throughout the early 1960s. The establishment of Students

Students protesting at the University of California, Berkeley, during the Free Speech movement in 1964

for a Democratic Society (SDS) at the University of Michigan in 1960 marked the beginning of organized student opposition to the domination of American life by big government and huge corporations: the "military-industrial complex." In 1964 students at the University of California, Berkeley, staged a sit-in involving thousands of protesters when the university chancellor banned political activities based around Telegraph Avenue. The chancellors act resulted in the formation of the Free Speech Movement (FSM), which organized a massive sit-in at the university's main administration building in December 1964.

The events at Berkeley soon spread to campuses across the country, and the focus of student protest shifted to opposition to American involvement in the war in Southeast Asia. The dramatic expansion of conscription meant that increasing numbers of young men confronted the prospect of fighting in Vietnam. In 1967 half a million protesters gathered in New York's Central Park to voice their opposition to the war and the draft by burning draft cards. The following spring, Columbia University was closed after violent confrontations between student activists and police; similar clashes occurred at Harvard, Cornell, and San Francisco State universities. Violent confrontations between protesters and the authorities came to a climax at the 1968 Democratic Party convention in Chicago when police clubbed and gassed protesters and bystanders alike. The Chicago riots encouraged extreme and violent elements within the protest movement, such as the Weathermen, who advocated revolutionary terrorism as their strategy and embarked on a campaign of bombings and killings before they were arrested. The antiwar movement lost its momentum in the early 1970s as President Nixon scaled down American involvement in the war, troops returned home, and the draft was ended.

THE U.S. MILITARY IN HAWAII

"We were climbing down to the boat, holding on to the face of the island in the dark, when a howling like wolves, like ghosts, came rising out of the island. 'Birds,' somebody said. 'The wind,' said someone else. But the air was still, and the high, clear sound wound like a ribbon around the island. It was, I know it, the island, the voice of the island singing, the sirens Odysseus heard.

"The Navy uses Kaho'olawe for bombing practice, not recognizing it as living, sacred earth. We had all heard it, the voice of our island singing."

Maxine Hong Kingston

From "Chinaman's Hat," in *Hawai'i One Summer* (Honolulu: University of Hawaii Press, 1998), p. 33.

Opposition to the draft and to the Vietnam War appear in various ways in Kingston's writing. In "The Brother in Vietnam" from *China Men,* for example, she explains strategies for avoiding the economy that supports the war: "The way to contribute less to the war was to go on welfare and eat out of garbage bins in back of grocery stores" (284–285). When Kingston and her husband, Earll, first moved to Hawaii, they attempted to live in a manner that did not contribute to the war economy. In *Hawai'i One Summer* she writes, "We did not look for new jobs in Hawai'i. It was the duty of the pacifist in a war economy not to work. When you used plastic wrap or made a phone call or drank grape juice or washed your clothes or drove a car, you ran the assembly lines that delivered bombs to Vietnam" (15). So the Kingstons ate out of supermarket garbage bins and found most of what they needed: "Shoes, clothes, tables, chairs washed up on the shores," she recalls (16). In *Tripmaster Monkey* the draft and Kingston's antidraft sympathies motivate Wittman's marriage to Taña while married men are still exempt from conscription. Conscription is one of the injustices from which the warrior woman seeks to liberate her villagers in *The Woman Warrior. Tripmaster Monkey* represents King-

KINGSTON ON WOMEN AND WORK

"In *Hawaii Over the Rainbow*, Kazuo Miya-moto says that in World War II relocation camps for Americans of Japanese ancestry, the women had the holiday of their lives—no cooking, no dishwashing. They felt more at leisure than back home because of the communal dining halls and camp kitchens. I can believe it."

Maxine Hong Kingston

From "Dishwashing," in *Hawai'i One Summer* (Honolulu: University of Hawaii Press, 1998), p. 24.

ston's experience of Berkeley in the 1960s, a time of extraordinary social and cultural change. She explains that she chose to tell a man's story because at that time, "A man had a much more dramatic life. . . . And then also, men had a more dangerous life, too, because they had the draft. They were always susceptible to having to go to Vietnam."[6]

The counterculture offered another means for disaffected youth to express their rejection of mainstream American values. The hippies who wore long hair, blue jeans, beads, and sandals and used mind-altering drugs such as LSD to achieve alternative states of consciousness shared the disillusionment of political activists but were also disillusioned with the concept of organized political action. Instead, they embraced an alternative lifestyle, based upon the psychologist Timothy Leary's credo: "turn on, tune in, drop out." Living in places such as San Francisco's Haight-Ashbury district, New York's East Village, or rural communes, hippies used hallucinogenic drugs and pursued forms of oriental mysticism such as meditation to achieve altered states of consciousness. The title *Tripmaster Monkey* reveals Kingston's understanding of 1960s counterculture. She explains: "Tripmaster was a word from the 1960s. People could be on acid, and there's a tripmaster who suggests trips for them and who guides them and keeps them from flipping out." She goes on to confess, "I feel that I myself was very good at doing that. Often I would be the one who would not take the drugs and the other people would take the drugs. I would make sure they were safe."[7] In the novel Wittman is approached at a party and asked if he will be the "tripmaster" for a group of people who are about to take LSD.

Kingston's political themes incorporate her pacifism, opposition to racism, and feminism. Feminism in America is commonly thought to have developed in two "waves." The first was the period leading up to and following from the 1848 Seneca Falls Convention, held in Seneca Falls, New York, at which the American suffragist movement was launched. Key thinkers and texts of this period include Margaret Fuller's *Woman in the Nineteenth Century* (1845), essays and speeches by Elizabeth Cady Stanton and Susan B. Anthony, and Charlotte Perkins Gilman's *Women and Economics* (1898). The second wave of

American feminism dates from the 1960s and marks the establishment of the modern women's movement. Key texts of second-wave feminism include Betty Friedan's *The Feminine Mystique* (1963), Shulamith Firestone's *The Dialectic of Sex* (1970), Kate Millett's *Sexual Politics* (1970), and Gloria Steinem's *Outrageous Acts and Everyday Rebellions* (1983). Kingston was a young student at Berkeley at the time of feminism's reemergence.

In reaction to the conservatism of the post–World War II years, the second wave of American feminism focused on male sexism and the domestic oppression of women. State and federal provision of childcare and the legalization of abortion formed part of the agenda of the National Organization for Women (NOW), founded by Friedan in 1966. In *The Feminine Mystique* Friedan called for women to renew the struggle of the first wave, which had culminated in female suffrage in 1920, but now feminist attention was focused on the exclusion of women from the public sphere and on sex-based discrimination in the workplace. Friedan's book documents the manifold ways in which the feminine mystique pervaded American culture and worked to keep women isolated both from their own feelings of dissatisfaction and frustration and also from sharing their common awareness that something was deeply wrong with their lives. Underlying the apparent problems with marriages, children, houses, and communities was the real problem of feminine entrapment. Friedan identified women's desire for something more than the domestic ideal that was equated with "true" femininity. Kingston belongs to the first generation of women who were able to escape the entrapment of the feminine mystique through education and professional work, though in *The Woman Warrior* she expresses her fear that her parents would force her into a traditional arranged marriage. The route of escape that she envisaged from such a marriage was education, using her intelligence to finance an independent lifestyle. In the book she shouts at her mother, "Do you know what the Teacher ghosts say about me? They tell me I'm smart, and I can win scholarships. I can get into colleges. I've already applied. I'm smart. I can do all kinds of things. I know how to get A's, and they say I could be a scientist or a mathematician if I want. I can make a living and take care of myself" (201). Rebellion of this

KINGSTON ON FEMINISM AND RACE

"I had no idea . . . how to make attraction selective, how to control its direction and magnitude. If I made myself American-pretty so that the five or six Chinese boys in the class fell in love with me, everyone else—the Caucasian, Negro, and Japanese boys—would too. Sisterliness, dignified and honorable, made much more sense."

Maxine Hong Kingston

From *The Woman Warrior: Memoirs of a Girlhood Among Ghosts* (New York: Knopf, 1976), p. 12.

Members of the National Organization for Women demonstrating at
the White House in the early 1970s

sort, based on the knowledge that an independent life for women was possible, was facilitated by the inroads made by the women's movement.

In the early 1970s, when Kingston was working on *The Woman Warrior,* positive legislative change affecting women's lives was under way. The Educational Amendments Act of 1972 made it mandatory for colleges to institute affirmative action programs regarding admissions, hiring, and athletic programs; Congress approved the Equal Rights Amendment to the Constitution in the same year and submitted it to the fifty state legislatures for ratification; and the landmark decision by the Supreme Court in *Roe v. Wade* (1973) overruled state laws forbidding abortions during the first three months of pregnancy. The Equal Rights Amendment, however, expired in 1982, having failed to gain ratification at the state level. Feminism came under attack for its failure to extend its sphere of interest beyond that of the middle class; divisions between moderate and radical feminists also undermined the unity of the movement and its ability to effect change. Political change is a fundamental motive of American feminism, but the concept of "change" articulated by different factions within the women's movement has varied from cultural revolution to radical separation of the sexes to liberal reforms of the existing socioeconomic order.

In the 1960s feminists called for equal rights, reproductive rights, and economic justice. The election of John F. Kennedy in 1960 helped to shift attitudes and to make social change appear more likely, and the formation of NOW meant that there was a new civil-rights group capable of lobbying government to enact and enforce legislation barring sex discrimination. This feminist agenda drew upon the relationship between the early women's movement, the New Left, and the Civil Rights movement. This relationship is described by Sara Evans in *Personal Politics* (1979). She counts the rise of Third World nationalism, the beatnik challenge to middle-class values, and growing racial unrest as the key social forces that contributed to the weakening of the structures of feminine oppression.

The second wave of feminism in America did little to acknowledge the interdependence of racism and sexism as symptomatic of a culture of oppression. Women of color were excluded from positions of public influence in both the black-male-dominated Civil Rights movement and the women's movement, which was dominated by white women. In *Feminist Theory: From Margin to Center* (1984) bell hooks criticizes the color (and class) blindness embedded in one of the resurgent feminist movement's canonical texts, Friedan's *The Feminine Mystique*. Hooks points out that Friedan "did not discuss who would be called in to take care of the children and maintain the home if more women like herself were freed from their house labor and given equal access with white men to the professions."[8] Not only black feminists such as Angela Davis and hooks but also all feminists of color insist upon recognition of the relationship between class and race as they crucially affect the experience of gender and sexualized power relationships. The complex interplay of race and gender relationships is Kingston's primary theme in both *The Woman Warrior* and *China Men*.

LIFESTYLE AND CULTURE

The society into which Kingston was born was the Chinese American community in Stockton and San Francisco. She describes the Chinese population of Stockton as small, tight-knit, and stable in that many people in the community came from the same village, Sun Woi, in China and tended not to move from Stockton once there. Their children have tended to remain in the town as well. As a consequence of this stability people know each other quite well, and the families share a common history. In contrast to the Chinese community of Hawaii, the Chinese people of Stockton live a more rural lifestyle, according to Kingston. She remarks, "People there [in Stockton] would work in the fields even if they lived in the city. There is more of a closeness to nature that way. In Hawaii . . . it's not like that. Hawaii feels more urban to me."[9]

The Kingstons moved from Berkeley to Hawaii in 1967 for two reasons. First was the desire to leave the mainland United States because they thought that by moving away they would be distancing themselves from the culture supporting the Vietnam War. More personally, they wanted to escape the violence of Berkeley and its drug culture. Kingston has repeatedly explained her commitment to the idea that protest cannot be divorced from action, even though she acknowledges that this requires time and so takes her away from her writing: "it takes a whole life to organize and demonstrate and it takes another whole life to get writing done."[10] In Berkeley in the 1960s she was protesting against the war in Vietnam; later she was involved in Asian American feminist, antinuclear, and antipornography protests. The attitude of dissent is strong in Kingston's character. Her commitment to the antiwar movement continues in her writing workshops with veterans of Vietnam and other wars. Reflecting upon her time in Hawaii in *Hawai'i One Summer,* Kingston observes, "looking back at Sanctuary at the Church of the Crossroads, I remember the AWOL soldiers who were true pacifist heroes" (xv).

Kingston did not visit China until 1984. She wanted to write down her imaginary version of the culture before she experienced the reality of life in China so that her vision would not be altered by her experience. In addition, her parents held ambivalent views of their native country and of what might happen to someone who returned. Kingston explains: "The older generation feels it's a very terrible place. If any of us go, something bad will happen to us. We will get killed or something. In my family, just about all the men were killed in the revolution. The other fear is that we'll be thought of as Communist sympathizers if we go and if there is a McCarthy type' witchhunt, we will be thrown in relocation camps. There is a whole weight of history involved here."[11] Thus, China represented a danger in itself, from which the Hongs had escaped, but it was also viewed as threatening the home that the family had found in the United States. Kingston recognizes, however, that this view is peculiar to the Chinese community in Stockton and is not a general attitude. She remarks that in this community, with its recent immigrants from Hong Kong as well as the older generation of people such as her parents, the idea of traveling for pleasure is not a part of the culture; rather, "Travel means desperately running from country to country."[12] When Kingston did visit China, she was gratified to find it was just as she had imagined it: "the colors, and the smells, the people, the faces, the incidents, were much as I had imagined. Many people said to me, 'Welcome home.' I did feel that I was going back to a place I had never been."[13] But even this experience was informed by the power of her creative imagination. Kingston speculates that the reason why her experience of China confirmed what she had written about it is that she was attuned to that reality; she was looking to find the China that she already knew in her imaginings. She explains, "It was accessible to me before I saw it, because I wrote it. The power of imagination leads us to what is real."[14] If what she found in China had been very different from the China represented in her writing, then it would have indicated that her imagination was not right, that it was failing to provide a bridge toward reality.

There is a complex relationship between fictional and historical cultures in Kingston's writing. She has been criticized for being unrepresentative of Chinese Americans, despite her repeated denials that she has ever sought to be representative of any group or community. When she asked one of her sisters how odd she would estimate their family and upbringing were, the sister guessed eight on a scale of one to ten, which Kingston takes to mean that theirs was not a representative family at all: "I am writing about one little village in the South of China and already in that little village they were not representative of all of the great, big China. And then those few people came to America and went to Stockton."[15] But she concedes that until there is a sufficient number of Chinese American authors in print, readers will have little with which to compare her work and see that what she has portrayed is her own unique way of viewing the world. This is what Kingston finds exciting and interesting—the encounter with people who are different from her, who present the possibility of being Chinese or indeed of being human in new and different ways.

The relationship between fiction and autobiography is not simple and straightforward in Kingston's work. Some critics have suggested that Kingston the writer should be identified with the figure of the woman warrior, even though it was her editor who suggested the title of her first book. When, some time later, the same editor suggested that she somehow "is" the woman warrior, Kingston's reaction was strongly negative. She does not identify herself with a figure whose military nature contrasts with her own pacifism, nor can she be identified in a simple one-to-one fashion with the characters she has created and whose stories she tells. Fiction is biographical in a new and innovative way in Kingston's work, as she recognizes: "what I've written are a new kind of biography . . . what I've written are biographies of imaginative people, and this is culturally correct, because this is the way my people are, my family. People come together and they tell each other their lives, and they make up the stories of their lives."[16] She locates the main concerns of her writing in the place where fantasy meets real life, "a blurred area, which is a border between [the] imagination and what actually happens."[17]

NOTES

1. Amy Ling, "Chinese American Women Writers: The Tradition Behind Maxine Hong Kingston," in *Redefining American Literary History,* edited by A. LaVonne Brown Ruoff and Jerry W. Ward Jr. (New York: Modern Language Association, 1990), p. 221.

2. Ibid., p. 219.

3. Maxine Hong Kingston, "Cultural Mis-readings by American Reviewers," in *Asian and Western Writers in Dialogue: New Cultural Identities,* edited by Guy Amirthanayagam (London: Macmillan, 1982), pp. 60–61.

4. Paul Skenazy, "Coming Home," in *Conversations with Maxine Hong Kingston,* edited by Skenazy and Tera Martin (Jackson: University of Mississippi Press), p. 114.

5. Kingston, "San Francisco's Chinatown: A View of the Other Side of Arnold Genthe's Camera," *American Heritage,* 30 (December 1978): 36.

6. Shelley Fisher Fishkin, "Interview with Maxine Hong Kingston," in *Conversations with Maxine Hong Kingston,* p. 166.

7. Neila C. Seshachari, "Reinventing Peace: Conversations with Tripmaster Maxine Hong Kingston," in *Conversations with Maxine Hong Kingston,* p. 204.

8. bell hooks, *Feminist Theory: From Margin to Center* (Boston: Beacon, 1984), pp. 1–2.

9. Karen Horton, "*Honolulu* Interview: Maxine Hong Kingston," in *Conversations with Maxine Hong Kingston,* p. 8.

10. Ibid., p. 9.

11. Ibid., p. 8.

12. Ibid., p. 9.

13. Paula Rabinowitz, "Eccentric Memories: A Conversation with Maxine Hong Kingston," in *Conversations with Maxine Hong Kingston,* pp. 70–71.

14. Ibid., p. 71.

15. Arturo Islas and Marilyn Yalom, "Interview with Maxine Hong Kingston," in *Conversations with Maxine Hong Kingston,* p. 22.

16. Kay Bonetti, "An Interview with Maxine Hong Kingston," in *Conversations with Maxine Hong Kingston,* p. 37.

17. Islas and Yalom, "Interview with Maxine Hong Kingston," p. 30.

The Woman Warrior: Memoirs of a Girlhood Among Ghosts. New York: Knopf, 1976.

Kingston's first book catapulted her from almost complete obscurity to sudden fame as the best-known Asian American writer of the late twentieth century. The book was variously praised as a feminist masterpiece and as a groundbreaking work of ethnic or multicultural literature. The narrative is divided into five interconnected stories: "No Name Woman," "White Tigers," "Shaman," "At the Western Palace," and "A Song for a Barbarian Reed Pipe." Each focuses upon a feminine figure—a female alter ego for the narrator. The stories are linked together by the authorial voice of Kingston as she recalls events from her childhood and the stories her mother, Brave Orchid, used to tell her. The stories are also connected by the dominant presence of Brave Orchid, whose stories, legends, and histories confront Kingston with an array of alternative female role models.

"No Name Woman" opens with Brave Orchid's admonition to keep secret the story she is about to tell. The adolescent Kingston then learns about her father's sister, the aunt she never knew she had because of the shameful circumstances of her death. Brave Orchid tells how her husband left her in China to work in America, the "Gold Mountain," with his father, brothers, and the husband of his sister. Some years later, Brave Orchid discovered that her sister-in-law had become pregnant even though her husband had been absent for a long time. The villagers also noticed, and on the night when the baby was due to be born, they raided the house, slaughtered the stock, and destroyed the harvest. The next morning, when she went to the well to fetch water, Brave Orchid found that her sister-in-law had drowned herself and her newborn child. The punishment of the No Name Woman continues even after her death, as the family refuses to acknowledge that she ever existed, but Brave Orchid tells the story to Kingston because, as she warns her, "Now that you have started to menstruate,

Kingston in 1983

what happened to her could happen to you. Don't humiliate us" (5). The narrator presents this story as an example of the kinds of stories her mother told her in order to teach her lessons or to warn her about life. They are also the stories that confused the young Kingston about the world in which she lived: the physical world of modern America, but also the emotional and psychological world of the China her immigrant parents left behind.

Kingston juxtaposes the stories of China, such as that of the No Name Woman, with details of her own childhood as she grew up in Stockton. In this way, she negotiates difficult questions: "how do you separate what is peculiar to childhood, to poverty, insanities, one family, your mother who marked your growing with stories, from what is Chinese? What is Chinese tradition and what is the movies?" (5–6). The narrator tries telling different versions of her aunt's story in order to make sense of it. Was the woman raped or seduced, or was she a romantic who, with her husband far away, fell in love with someone else? Or was she an adventurer who, denied the opportunity her brothers had to travel because of her gender, chose to cross other boundaries instead? Kingston compares herself with the No Name Woman: Did her aunt try to make herself attractive? Did she suffer because of the unequal treatment of boys and girls in Chinese culture? Important from Kingston's point of view is her mother's role in the aunt's punishment and death. Did Brave Orchid join the other villagers in the raid, participating in her sister-in-law's punishment, just as she demands her daughter participate in the ongoing punishment by keeping silent about the story? The narrative begins, then, with the breaking of this silence, though Kingston suspects that her aunt's ghost is not necessarily a benevolent influence that haunts her and her writing: "I am telling on her, and she was a spite suicide, drowning herself in the drinking water" (16).

The next story, "White Tigers," introduces the figure of the warrior woman: "When we Chinese girls listened to the adults talk-story, we learned that we failed if we grew up to be but wives or slaves. We could be heroines, swordswomen" (19). Kingston learned about these warrior women from her mother's storytelling, from the dreams she experienced as the stories sent her off to sleep, and from the Chinese movies she watched every Sunday. Through the story of the warrior woman she realizes the power of her mother's storytelling, which has given her the role model of the warrior woman and made it possible for her to imagine herself in this role. In the story Kingston projects herself into the figure of Fa Mu Lan, reliving her years of training, military career, and her act of disguising herself as a man in order to lead troops into battle. The description of Fa Mu Lan's training in mystical as well as physical skills introduces magical and fantastic elements into the narrative. The narrator says that her training will be complete when she can "point at the sky and make a sword appear, a silver bolt in the sunlight, and control its slashing with my mind" (33). She spends time alone in the mountains of the white tigers, enduring a test of survival, when she experiences a mystical vision; she learns the skills of killing from the tigers, but she also

THE WOMAN WARRIOR

"My father first brushed the words in ink, and they fluttered down my back row after row. Then he began cutting; to make fine lines and points he used thin blades, for the stems, large blades.

"My mother caught the blood and wiped the cuts with a cold towel soaked in wine. It hurt terribly—the cuts sharp; the air burning; the alcohol cold, then hot—pain so various. I gripped my knees. I released them. Neither tension nor relaxation helped. I wanted to cry. If not for the fifteen years of training I would have writhed on the floor; I would have had to be held down. The list of grievances went on and on. If an enemy should flay me, the light would shine through my skin like lace."

Maxine Hong Kingston

From *The Woman Warrior: Memoirs of a Girlhood Among Ghosts* (New York: Knopf, 1976), pp. 34-35.

needs the wisdom of dragons. By looking into a gourd of water, she is able to witness the acts of cruelty and injustice that she will eventually avenge. In an echo of "No Name Woman," she sees the faces of the bandits who raid and steal from their neighbors, and she watches as "fat men sat on naked little girls. I watched powerful men count their money, and starving men count theirs" (30). Reflected in the gourd she also sees an army of horsemen arrive in her village to take one conscript from each family, including her husband and brother.

When her training is complete, the warrior woman returns to her village to take the place of her father, who has finally been conscripted. Before she leaves to join her army, however, her parents carve into the flesh of her back a list of all the grievances of their family and their village: "'Wherever you go, whatever happens to you, people will know our sacrifice,' my mother said. . . . She meant that even if I got killed, the people could use my dead body for a weapon . . .'" (34). The army of peasants that she leads does not rape and plunder; instead, she brings order and peace all the way to the capital, where the corrupt emperor is overthrown. She then returns to her village to exact revenge upon the local baron or warlord who has stolen food and children from the villagers.

The life of the warrior woman represents what the narrator calls "perfect filiality": she is the perfect daughter. Compared with her, Kingston views her American achievements as disappointing. What are A grades compared to rescuing a village from a tyrannical warlord? She is afraid that when her parents return to China, as she fears they will, they will sell her into slavery unless she proves to them her value. But the whole issue of feminine value is difficult for the narrator to understand. She overhears her parents and their neighbors repeating traditional sayings about the worthlessness of girls: "Feeding girls is feeding cowbirds. . . . When you raise girls, you're raising children for strangers" (46). This devaluation of girls arises from the perception that a girl will leave her family when she marries, and all that has been invested in her upbringing will be transferred to her husband's family. Kingston explains: "It was said, 'There is an outward tendency in females,' which meant that I was getting straight A's for the good of my future husband's family, not my own" (47). She goes on to tell how she might give expression to the character of the warrior woman, who drives her to resist the negative images of women with which she is surrounded. She will not have a husband, she will always work to support herself, and she will fight the forces of corruption around her: "It's not just the stupid racists that I have to do something about, but the tyrants who for whatever reason deny my family food and work" (49).

The private injustices suffered by her family, as well as the cultural injustices of racism and sexism, require the warrior woman's attention. But Kingston admits to confusion about the glories of combat: in China the Communists have killed members of her own family rather than the corrupt barons, and in Stockton, the fighting she has witnessed has "not been glorious but slum grubby" (51). At the end of the story, however, she acknowledges the similarity between herself and the warrior woman. They are both seeking revenge, but Kingston will have her vengeance by writing of the injustices she has both suffered and witnessed: "The reporting is the vengeance—not the beheading, not the gutting, but the words" (53).

"Shaman" tells of Kingston's mother's life in China as she waited for her husband to send for her to join him in America. In the story Brave Orchid uses the money her husband sends her to pay for her training as a doctor and obstetrician. While at college she deals with the ghost that haunts one of the rooms in which no one will sleep. This demonstration of her courage and determination is represented by the narrator as indicative of Brave Orchid's "dragon" quality: "She could make herself not weak. During danger she fanned out her dragon claws and riffled her red sequin scales and unfolded her coiling green stripes" (67). She does battle with the ghost and then leads the young women, her fellow students, in a final onslaught against the ghost. After graduation she returns to her village and is greeted with triumph and great celebration: "She had gone away ordinary and come back miraculous, like the ancient magicians who came down from the mountains" (76).

In this way Brave Orchid is reminiscent of the woman warrior, vanquishing evil and returning to her village triumphant. But among the purchases she makes to celebrate her graduation, Brave Orchid buys a slave girl. Her mother's participation in the devaluation of girls bothers

Kingston, who plies her mother with questions about how much she paid for the slave, how much other types of slaves were sold for, and how much Brave Orchid paid the hospital when she was born. She goes on to wonder whether her mother participated further in the misogynistic practices of her culture, such as female infanticide. By telling the stories of her experiences in China, Brave Orchid lends her daughter nightmare visions of dead and deformed babies, ghosts, and other monsters, so that Kingston must divide her life into "American-normal" and the monstrous Chinese images, reserved for "the language of impossible stories" (87). The narrator repeats a series of the ghost stories that Brave Orchid told. After she joins her husband in America, Brave Orchid must deal with the foreign "ghosts" who people her new home: "Taxi Ghosts, Bus Ghosts, Police Ghosts, Fire Ghosts, Meter Reader Ghosts, Tree Trimming Ghosts, Five-and-Dime Ghosts" (97). In America she works night and day in the laundry, doing demeaning physical work quite unlike her medical practice in China. But still she triumphs and passes on to her daughter this same capacity for courage and determination, as Kingston acknowledges: "I am really a Dragon, as she is a Dragon, both of us born in dragon years" (109).

In contrast to Brave Orchid, who has all the personal qualities required to survive in China and in America, her sister Moon Orchid is delicate, fragile, and feminine. "At the Western Palace" tells Moon Orchid's story. It begins with the contrast between Brave Orchid, who sits in the airport awaiting her sister's arrival and concentrating to keep the airplane safely in the air by sheer power of will, and Moon Orchid, who stands in the immigration line laughing at nothing. The narrator tells in detail the story of Brave Orchid's efforts to make her sister assert her Chinese rights over the husband who has lived in America with his American second wife and their children for more than thirty years: "Claim your rights. Those are *your* children. He's got two sons. *You* have two sons. You take them away from her. You become their mother," Brave Orchid urges her sister (125). But Moon Orchid and her daughter are what Brave Orchid calls "the lovely useless type" (128): they are not strong like her. The narrator details the ways in which Moon Orchid fails to adapt to the new lifestyle of her sister and her family. The circumstances of her confrontation with the husband she has not seen for thirty years produce a kind of slapstick comedy, with Brave Orchid sending her son to the husband's office under the pretext that there has been an accident and his medical assistance is needed. The rejection that Moon Orchid suffers at her husband's hands and the humiliation of being told by him that she and her daughter have become, in his words, "people in a book I read long ago" (154) emphasize the sense of alienation, of not belonging, that she has experienced since arriving in America. She develops the paranoid delusion that Mexicans are plotting against her life and, despite all of Brave Orchid's doctoring, retreats deeper and deeper into madness.

The final story in the collection, "A Song for a Barbarian Reed Pipe," begins by undercutting the veracity of the preceding story. The narrator first gives her brother's sketchy account as a witness to the confrontation between Moon Orchid and her estranged husband, but then she admits that in fact her brother told the story to one of their sisters, who in turn transmitted it to Kingston. The preceding story, therefore, is reduced to the level of invention rather than reported fact. In this final story the theme of storytelling comes to the fore. Kingston describes how her mother cut her frenum (the piece of flesh anchoring the tongue) in order to prevent her from becoming tongue-tied. She confesses that she needed this help because when she went to school and had to speak English for the first time, she became silent. She was struck dumb for years, but so too were her sister and several other Chinese girls she met at school. After American school, she went to Chinese school in the evening, where the girls were not mute.

Kingston relates her silence to the conflicting demands placed upon her by Chinese and American cultures. Her parents make use of her voice to translate for them without realizing that while she can translate the words, she cannot translate across the cultural gap. This difficulty is illustrated by a story about a delivery boy who mistakenly delivers medicine to the laundry. Brave Orchid interprets this as a curse; he has brought illness into their family and threatened their health and their future. She sends Kingston to the drugstore to demand "reparation candy" (170), something sweet to dispel the curse brought upon the household. But her daughter does not have the words to explain the complexities of this situation, and the druggist simply assumes that she is begging for free candy. Brave Orchid, however, believes she has taught the druggist a lesson. Conflicting demands are made even on the timbre of Kingston's voice: Chinese women's voices are "strong and bossy" but the "American-Chinese" girls try to cultivate soft, whispering voices that are "American feminine" (172). She tells of her hostility toward one particular Chinese girl who does not speak even in Chinese school and represents everything that she fears and rejects in herself. This hatred culminates in the episode in which she attempts to beat the silent girl into talking. The consequence is, however, that Kingston is confined to bed with a mysterious hysterical illness for the next eighteen months.

Kingston's difficulty speaking is related also to the way language is used by the Chinese American community. Chinese immigrants routinely mislead American authorities in order to protect themselves against the forces of institutionalized racism. Obscure Chinese rituals and traditions are practiced by her parents, who refuse to explain the significance of their actions, and the children are punished for breaking taboos of which they know nothing. Then there are all those things of which the Chinese never speak: Kingston remarks, "If we had to depend upon being told, we'd have no religion, no babies, no menstruation (sex, of course, unspeakable), no death" (185). Language is used for complex purposes of which the young narrator has little understanding. She does recognize that "talking and not talking made the difference between sanity and insanity" (186) because this characterizes the unstable women who live in the neighborhood, such as Crazy Mary or the "witchwoman," nicknamed Pee-A-Nah. Kingston's fear is that, since every family appears to have an unbalanced woman to care for, she is the one who will be the crazy woman in her family. This concern is based on the deeper fear that her parents will sell her as a slave; later, when it becomes apparent that they have postponed thoughts of returning to China, she is afraid they will arrange a marriage for her. Her response to these fears is to make herself as undesirable as possible so that nobody will want to buy her or marry her. Eventually, she has saved up hundreds of grievances that she must tell her mother, and they escape her in an uncontrolled outburst; her mother denies her sense of grievance, telling her that she is unable to distinguish reality from invention, that they never intended to marry her off, and that she cannot take a joke.

"A Song for a Barbarian Reed Pipe" ends with a story that Kingston shares with her mother: "The beginning is hers, the ending is mine" (206). She tells of her grandmother in China, who loved the theater so much that she insisted the entire household attend with her, even though robbers habitually raided houses in the area during theater performances. One night bandits struck, but they raided the theater rather than the family's house. The family, luckily, was unharmed, and they returned to their home, which was untouched, "proof to my grandmother that our family was immune to harm as long as they went to plays" (207). The saving nature of literature, of creative expression, is dramatized by the story of Ts'ai Yen, a poetess who is kidnapped by barbarians and kept hostage for twelve years. When she is ransomed and returned to her people, she brings back with her the songs she has sung of her loneliness and longing for her family. These songs, which also capture some of the sadness and anger expressed by the barbarians as they played their reed pipes, were sung to the accompaniment of Chinese instruments. The narrator comments of one song in particular, "It translated well" (209); the common experience of sadness and longing united the Chinese and the barbarians through the medium of poetry. In the same way Kingston's stories unite the Chinese and the American aspects of her experience.

China Men. New York: Knopf, 1980.

Kingston's second book is organized into six named sections: "The Father from China," "The Great Grandfather of the Sandalwood Mountains," "The Grandfather of the Sierra Nevada Mountains," "The Making of More Americans," "The American Father," and "The Brother in Vietnam." Each of these sections ends with one or two short stories based on traditional Chinese myths. Kingston uses the technique of juxtaposition to suggest points of relevant contrast between the histories she gives and the mythical stories. The book begins with two short, mythic stories: "On Discovery" and "On Fathers." The first describes the arrival of a man named Tang Ao in the Land of Women. He must be prepared before he can meet the queen, and his preparation is described in detail: his ears are pierced, his toes are broken, and his feet bound; the hairs are plucked from his face and his face is painted. The story ends with the suggestion that this mythical Land of Women is in fact in North America. "On Discovery" serves as an introduction to the entire book in two ways: first, it gives an account of the mutilation of women's bodies in male-dominated Chinese society, which is made more disturbing by Kingston's reversal of the gender roles in having women mutilate Tang Ao's body. Second, the story stands as a complex metaphor for the experience of emasculation suffered by Chinese immigrant men in America. That is, these men left the patriarchal society of China, in which they were powerful and occupied the dominant position, to come to the United States, where racism reduced them to a position of almost "feminine" powerlessness.

"On Fathers" opens with the young narrator, based loosely on Kingston herself, waiting with her brothers and sisters at the gate before their house for their father to come home and mistaking a stranger for him. As the stranger walks away, they realize it was his suit and shoes, so like their father's, that confused them. The section that follows, "The Father from China," develops this perception that the narrator has not been able really to know her father. She remembers times when he played with her and her siblings, but most of her memories are of his anger, the children's fear, and the stream of obscenities he would utter that were demeaning to women. She also recalls the times when her father was

Maxine Hong Kingston

author of *The Woman Warrior*

CHINAMEN

Dust jacket for Kingston's second book, published in 1980, which recounts the experiences of her father and other male relatives

cheated by gypsy women and hopes it is only these women, not women in general, whom he regards as obscene. But these are only her speculations. Her father would scream wordlessly in the night, and for weeks and months would go silent, leaving the family to guess at the terrible things that caused this silence and the complete rejection of China: "No stories. No past. No China. You only look and talk Chinese" (14). And so the narrator must challenge her father to tell her the truth if she has guessed wrong: "I'll tell you what I suppose from your silences and few words, and you can tell me that I'm mistaken. You'll just have to speak up with the real story if I've got you wrong" (15).

The narrative then turns to the details of Kingston's father's early life in China. From his birth he is destined to be a scholar and to take the imperial examinations. But his father, Ah Goong, is disappointed to have yet another son when he longed for a daughter. Ah Goong dotes on a baby girl who was born in the village at the same time as his son, and he is sad that because of her gender she had no party to welcome her, no fine clothes, and no toys. So he exchanges his baby son for her. When his wife discovers that her baby son is gone and that her husband has exchanged him for a worthless girl, she is furious, accusing him of madness and idiocy, "trading a boy for a slave" (21), and calling the girl's family thieves and swindlers. After this incident, the boy's mother, Ah Po, keeps him close to her. BaBa, as he is called, is teased by his brothers for his love of studying, and they exclude him from their games. At the age of fourteen he leaves the village to take the imperial examinations. This gives BaBa his first experience of the larger world and of a community of scholars. Though he does not excel, he wins a position as village teacher.

The narrator describes the circumstances of her parents' marriage, the ceremony, and the accompanying rituals in detail. Kingston's father's career as the village schoolteacher is not successful; his pupils fail to appreciate the learning of their teacher and misbehave. For his part,

BaBa has no patience with these students, and gradually he becomes susceptible to the stories he hears of the Gold Mountain, America. Eventually, he determines to go there himself to make his fortune, but that requires that he learn how to deal with the U.S. immigration officials in order to obtain a legal visa. Kingston concedes that her father never told the story of his journey to America, nor how he came to enter the country, and so she must invent the story that might have happened.

Kingston's father's life in New York, working in the laundry he operates with three friends and becoming familiar with the city, changes when his wife writes to tell him that their two children have died and that he should return immediately. Instead, he instructs her to improve her education and obtain a degree, telling her that when she has done these things he will send for her to join him. Thus, after fifteen years apart, they are reunited. But shortly afterward, the three friends draw up deeds for the laundry business and establish a partnership from which Kingston's father is excluded. He is cheated out of his share in the laundry where he has worked so hard, so with his wife he leaves New York for California to begin again.

The history of Kingston's father's life before he settled in Stockton, California, is juxtaposed with a mythical story, "The Ghostmate," in which a young man returns from having taken the imperial examinations. He is caught in a fierce storm and seeks shelter in a great house in the woods. The woman who lives in the house is the most beautiful woman he has ever seen, and she entices him to stay with her. Gradually, he forgets the wife and family to whom he was returning, but when he eventually leaves, everyone who sees him flees in fright as from a ghost. He discovers, where the great house had been, the grave marker of a noblewoman who has been dead for years. The story ends with the observation, "Fancy lovers never last" (81).

"The Great Grandfather of the Sandalwood Mountains" begins with Kingston's experience of sending money in response to begging letters from her surviving relatives in China and the conflicting stories she has heard about life in China since the Revolution. She admits to a powerful desire to visit China, to know the people: "I want to talk to Cantonese, who have always been revolutionaries, nonconformists, people with fabulous imaginations, people who invented the Gold Mountain. I

KINGSTON ON HER FATHER

"When my father was a young man, working in a laundry on Mott Street in New York, he and his partners raced at meals. Last one to finish eating washed the dishes. They ate fast."

Maxine Hong Kingston

From "Dishwashing," in *Hawai'i One Summer* (Honolulu: University of Hawaii Press, 1998), p. 22.

want to discern what makes people go West and turn into Americans" (87). In the ensuing history of her great-grandfather, Bak Goong, who traveled to Hawaii (the Sandalwood Mountains) and in her own experience of living there she seeks the imaginative answers to these questions. She tells how Bak Goong was recruited in China by the Royal Hawaiian Agricultural Society on a three-year contract to work in the sugar industry. Kingston rehearses the fine promises made by the agent and compares them first with the conditions of Bak Goong's sea passage and then with the harsh reality of the work he is to do. Where he had expected to find a sugarcane plantation, he finds wilderness, out of which it is his job to hack and clear farmland. The heat, dust, and thirst are bad enough, but the enforced silence is too much for him to bear. Kingston describes in detail the harsh conditions, the heavy work he must perform, and the talk-story that enables the Chinese laborers to endure. Bak Goong's story ends with a "shout party" (118) that changes the quality of their lives by challenging the white demon overseers to stop them from talking, singing, and shouting. The section ends with two mythical stories. The first, "On Mortality," tells of Tu Tzu-chun, who is reborn three times, each time squandering the wishes that are given him. He has to work to repay a Taoist monk who has given him a potion that evokes dreams and images, but he is forbidden to make any noise. Tu Tzu-chun manages to repress all sounds until at last he utters a gasp and finds that he has spoiled the elixir of immortality that the monk had been creating for the human race. The second story, "On Mortality Again," tells of the efforts of Maui, the Polynesian trickster god, to obtain immortality for the human race.

"The Grandfather of the Sierra Nevada Mountains" is the story of Kingston's paternal grandfather, Ah Goong, and his three journeys to America to work on the building of the railroads. She describes how he worked to clear the route of the tracks by dynamiting trees, building bridges, filling ravines, and digging tunnels through the mountains. Ah Goong endured the misery of the cold winters and the ever-present danger of death by falling, handling explosives, or avalanches caused by the explosions: "They lost count of the number dead; there is no record of how many died building the railroad. Or maybe it was demons doing the counting and chinamen not worth counting" (138). Kingston describes the Chinese men's strike to demand decent working conditions and pay and equality with white workers; their slogan is "Eight hours a day good for white man, all the same good for China Man" (141). Though the strike wins at least a compromise, the Chinese railroad workers know that there is no equality between them and the whites. The triumph the

Chinese share upon completion of the transcontinental railroad is tainted by the awareness that they must move on: "The Driving Out had begun" (145). Thus, Ah Goong lives the life of a drifter, constantly moving from place to place but keeping clear of towns and settlements from which he might be driven out, killed, or lynched, as many other Chinese have been. Finally, after he has returned one more time to the United States, his family sends for him to return to China.

Ah Goong's story is followed by a chronological account of the anti-Chinese laws that institutionalized the violent racism he sought to escape. In "The Laws" Kingston sets out the legislation that regulated and limited both the entry of Chinese into the United States and their ability to apply for citizenship. These were legislative and judicial attempts to prevent the permanent settlement of those Chinese who traveled to America to work. This factual and historical account is followed by "Alaska China Men," a story about how those Chinese who traveled to Alaska to work in gold mining were forcibly "shipped out" (160).

"The Making of More Americans" begins with Kingston's recollections of her "grandfathers" (a term used loosely for any older male ancestor) and then gives her account of Sahm Goong's haunting by the ghost of his brother, Say Goong. The ghost is dispelled when his brother orders him to go home: "Go back to China. Go now. To China" (170); then Sahm Goong himself disappears, "perhaps going back to China, perhaps dead here like his brother" (171). But when relatives come to visit the place where the two grandfathers had lived, they call the place "ancestral ground" (171) in recognition of the grandfathers and their contribution to the nation. One of Sahm Goong's grandsons lives a successful American life but is sent letters by his mother in China urging him to return, sell his daughters, apprentice his son, and marry a second wife. Gradually, the letters change and beg first for money and then for food, telling of famine and terrible hunger. Finally, his mother's ghost haunts him, tormenting him with accusations and blaming him for her death. He tries scolding her, as Sahm Goong had done to his brother's ghost, but that is ineffectual. Only when he travels to China and escorts his mother's ghost to her grave, where he performs all the necessary rituals, is he able to appease the ghost and return home to America to live as he had before. Another grandfather is Kau Goong, the brother of Kingston's grandmother and a former riverboat pirate; he dies in Stockton some years after deciding that he will not return to China because America is his home. Kingston gives a detailed description of his funeral, but when she asks her parents about the rituals, she is told, "We treat Kau

Goong and any other grandfathers who may be in that cemetery like any American dead" (189).

Whereas Kau Goong decides that he belongs in America, Uncle Bun eventually decides to return to China. Kingston tells about his increasing paranoia, his delusion that he will be punished for his Communist sympathies, and his decision to go back to his village in China, where he will not be poisoned or made to eat garbage, as he fears is the case in America. Like the aunt Kingston meets in San Francisco, who tells of her suffering although she does not want to hear about it, she concedes, "I did have a duty to hear it and remember it" (207). The story of the aunt and her husband, I Fu, who have earned and lost several fortunes, is followed by that of Kingston's mother's brother, who lives in Singapore. Brave Orchid is disappointed, after speaking on the telephone with her brother for the first time in fifty years, that they were unable to say anything significant to each other.

"The Making of More Americans" ends with two stories: "The Wild Man of the Green Swamp," about a Chinese man who is discovered living in a swamp in Florida, and "The Adventures of Lo Bun Sun," about a Chinese version of Robinson Crusoe. The Wild Man lives in the swamp because he refuses to return to China, but he is also too homesick to settle happily in the United States. Kingston's mother tells the story of Lo Bun Sun's shipwreck, the daily routines for survival that he establishes, and how after twenty-five years on an island he rescues a captive from a group of cannibals who are about to kill and eat him. Lo Bun Sun (Kingston's transcription of *Robinson* pronounced with a Chinese accent) names the freed captive Sing Kay Ng, "because I saved your life on a Friday" (231), and together they have a series of adventures before Lo Bun Sun returns to the land of his birth.

"The American Father" begins with the narrator's attempt to match her father's official history with what she knows of his life. Thus, according to his papers, he was born in San Francisco in 1903, which means that his mother "gave birth at a distance" or else "the men of those days had the power to have babies" (237). Not only was he born at a distance, he was also married at a distance, since he was actually born and married in China. In this way, Kingston indicates that she is concerned with her father's life in America. She describes the places that appeared to her to be special "father places" (240) and recalls accompanying him to work and helping to prepare the gambling house he managed. She tells of how her parents left New York after being cheated out of their share of the laundry business and went to Stockton, their fares paid for by a man from their village in China. Her father worked in the gambling house while her mother worked as the owner's family's servant. After the gambling house is closed, BaBa becomes disheartened and depressed. He sits all day, nagged by his wife to find a job, until finally the children's wildness causes him to go out and find work. At this time he buys a laundry in Stockton and his "liveliness" returns (254). The section ends with "The Li Sao: An Elegy." This is the story of Ch'ü Yüan, or Ch'ü P'ing, who is banished from the Chou Kingdom because he offered the king the unpopular advice that he should not fight a losing war. He wanders the kingdom, lamenting his fall from power and having many adventures, but in all his travels he never met a person who was not corrupt. Finally, Ch'ü Yüan drowns himself in a river; only then do the people realize what they have lost, and they try unsuccessfully to call him back.

China Men concludes with the section titled "The Brother in Vietnam." Kingston tells of her early awareness of World War II, the images in a war movie, photographs in magazines of people killed in the fighting, and cartoons in Chinese magazines of the Japanese killing and torturing American soldiers and Chinese civilians. She recalls that many men left China for the Gold Mountain in order to escape conscription: "The Gold Mountain does not make war, is not invaded, and has no draft. The government does not capture men and boys and send them to war" (269), they reasoned. Kingston's father and uncles were of the age to be conscripted when they left China; even in America, they had techniques for eluding the draft by making themselves appear to be ill. Her father escapes the draft by failing the medical examination because his wife has been using her medical knowledge to poison him. After the war the cousins who were soldiers and the Japanese Americans who had been sent to relocation camps never speak of their experiences. Kingston recalls hearing of the Communist Revolution in China, wearing dog tags at school during the Korean War, and fearing that the Vietnam War would involve a conflict between Chinese Americans and the Chinese in which her own brothers would be involved. She describes the choice one of her brothers

THE END OF THE VIETNAM WAR

"The war is more or less over, but we have remained here. The military paraphernalia also remains; even our dovish members of Congress have defended Hawai'i against military cuts. But after ten years in these islands, I see through camouflages and find the winding trails inland, away from the rim. Reading [Paul] Goodman's Hawai'i poems now, I hardly understand why he wanted plain loves; the world calmer, I like complexities. That his sadness seems inappropriate shows the possibility of a happier place, Hawai'i a vacation spot. I want to stay for a while to vacation."

Maxine Hong Kingston

From "War," in *Hawai'i One Summer* (Honolulu: University of Hawaii Press, 1998), p. 19.

must make between going to Canada to evade the draft and enlisting in the navy. He chooses to enlist, reasoning that "he would be a Pacifist in the Navy rather than in jail, no more or less guilty than the ordinary stay-at-home citizen of the war economy" (285). Kingston tells of her brother's training, the places he visits as a communications expert on an aircraft carrier, and his return home, glad that he survived without killing anyone. The book ends with a story called "The Hundred-Year-Old Man" and Kingston's reflections in "On Listening," in which she tells of the versions of the Gold Mountain legend she hears at a party and suggests that there is no definitive narrative of the Chinese experience in America.

Hawai'i One Summer, 1978. San Francisco: Meadow Press, 1987. Republished as *Hawaii One Summer.* Honolulu: University of Hawaii Press, 1998.

Kingston's third book is a collection of short prose pieces, all but one of which were originally published in 1978 in Kingston's "Hers" column in *The New York Times.* She was completing *China Men* at the time and describes these essays as her way of taking a break from writing the book. The essays were published in a limited, hand-printed edition by Leigh McLellan of Meadow Press in San Francisco, with original woodblock prints by Deng Ming-Dao, the son of the author Jade Snow Wong. In the preface to the University of Hawaii Press edition (1998) Kingston explains that she wrote the essays in the middle of her seventeen-year sojourn in Hawaii. She had intended to leave the state out of her considerations, describing how she felt an outsider there, even though some of her great-grandfathers and her paternal grandfather had lived and worked in Hawaii: "I felt the kapu—these are not your stories to write; these myths are not your myths; the Hawaiians are not your people. You are haole" (xii). Kingston felt excluded not only from the Hawaiian community but also from the local literary culture: "it did not feel good to be a writer in a place that is not a writing culture, where written language is only a few hundred years old. The literary community in Hawai'i argues over who owns the myths and stories, whether the local language and writings should be exported to the Mainland, whether or not so-and-so is authentic, is Hawaiian" (xi–xii). Consequently, Kingston wrote about California and China, about experiences that were personal to her and her family. But still Hawaii enters the essays, in the descriptions of the sea, air, and landscapes, and in the history that determines the quality of contemporary life in Hawaii.

The impetus for writing these diary-like pieces in the summer of 1978 was an invitation to the twentieth-year reunion of Kingston's high-school class and the reflections to which the invitation gave rise. She begins with her and her husband's purchase of their first house in Hawaii early in 1978 and the changes this event brought about in how she thought of herself: "The brain automatically adds 20 years of mortgage to one's age. And *mortgage* derives from *mors, mortis,* as in *mortal*" (4). In contrast, while they had rented, she "didn't need to own land to belong on this planet" (3). Kingston describes the manner in which she, her husband, Earll, and her son, Joseph, made the new house feel like home. But she concludes that the final reason why they were able to live in this house was the promise that if the responsibility of ownership should prove too burdensome, they could sell.

In "My High School Reunion" Kingston again writes about feelings and the changes in her emotional life. The prospect of attending the twentieth-year reunion reminds her of why she stayed away from the tenth reunion, but she admits, "I've been having dreams about the people in high school, and wake up with an urge to talk to them, find out how they turned out" (9). She recalls stories she has heard about the reunions of friends and family; she remembers the interpersonal dynamics of high-school cliques, groups, and gangs; and she imagines what an ideal reunion would be like: "It would be nice to go to a reunion where we look at one another and know without explanations how much we improved in twenty years of life. And know that we had something to do with one another's outcomes, companions in time for a while, lucky to meet again" (13).

"War" recounts the Kingstons' move from California and their first years in Hawaii. They moved from the mainland to protest America's involvement in the Vietnam War but found when they arrived in Hawaii that instead of escape from the war, they had come as close as one could get to it while remaining in the United States. In Hawaii the Kingstons heard the U.S. military's target practice, saw the flag-draped coffins, and met the soldiers on R and R ("rest and recreation"). They continued their protest, as well as they could, by assisting the soldiers who had gone AWOL. More recently, although the signs of Hawaii's military role are still to be found, Kingston has seen the islands returning to their peacetime character as a vacation resort and a place of great natural beauty. Juxtaposed with these reflections on war and peace is the essay "Dishwashing," which takes a much more mundane activity as its theme. Kingston is soon led to deeper issues, however, such as the importance of order in one's life and how one's approach to cleaning and dishwashing reflects

KINGSTON ON NATURE

"A city person encountering nature hardly recognizes it, has no patience for its cycles, and disregards animals and plants unless they roar and exfoliate in spectacular aberrations. Preferring the city myself, I can better discern natural phenomena when books point them out; I also need to verify what I think I've seen, even though charts of phyla and species are orderly whereas nature is wild, unruly."

Maxine Hong Kingston

From "A City Person Encountering Nature," in *Hawai'i One Summer* (Honolulu: University of Hawaii Press, 1998), p. 35.

changing emotional states. She speculates, "If I can solve dishwashing, I can solve life and suicide. . . . [D]ishwashing is important. A life-and-death matter, to be dealt with three times a day" (25).

In "Chinaman's Hat" Kingston writes about the experience of living in Hawaii. Her thoughts focus upon Mokoli'i Island, which is clearly visible from the island on which she lives, Oahu, and which is commonly called Chinaman's Hat because of the obvious resemblance between the shapes. Kingston describes her shock when she first heard this name and admits that she expected other racial slurs to follow. But they did not. Although the channel that separates Oahu and Chinaman's Hat is a spawning place for sharks, three times she swam out to the island. These recollections remind her of the almost mystical nature of Hawaii—the way the islands deceive humans into believing they are safe, the way the air "breathes warm on the skin," and the way the wind sounds like "the voice of the island singing, the sirens Odysseus heard" (33). Kingston continues this theme in "A City Person Encountering Nature," in which she tells of her discovery of the extraordinary natural sights she encountered in Hawaii and her impulse to name the seemingly mysterious things that she found. "Strange Sightings" returns to the mystical view of Hawaii and the idea that "spiritual forces converge at Hawai'i, as do ocean currents and winds" (52). Kingston reports that she has seen a "whirling witch," that Earll has seen a little witch dancing on his dresser, that Joseph has seen a Menehune, "one of the little people of Hawai'i" (55), and that other friends have seen supernatural sights.

In "Useful Education" Kingston considers the relationship between her writing and her education. She recalls her fourth-grade teacher, who required the children to make a book called "Gems" in which they copied the words she wrote on the blackboard. She recalls teaching her own students to write by allowing them to write what they please, though she concedes this method is inimical to the organized nature of modern education and so has taught essay-writing as well, so that her students would be able to survive college. Ultimately, however, she remembers how tough writers are, how resistant they are to bad teaching: "Kwan Kung, the god of war and literature, rides before us"

(45). Kingston considers the nature of writers in "Talk Story: A Writers' Conference," which describes the first conference ever held for Asian American and Hawaiian writers. She recalls how, listening to the speakers at the conference, she felt an outsider among the Hawaiian literary community, "a Captain Cook of literature, plundering the islands for metaphors, looting images, distorting the landscape with a mainland—mainstream—viewpoint" (47). But then Kingston tells of a confrontation between Chinese American men and women at the meeting. Two panelists argued "that publishers maintain a ghetto of female ethnic autobiographers and reject the work of male ethnic novelists" (48), to which the Chinese American women and other feminists violently objected. Kingston also writes that listening to the work of other authors at the conference disturbed the rhythms of her creativity.

"Lew Welch: An Appreciation" is the one essay in the collection that was not published in *The New York Times*. In this piece Kingston writes about the achievement of this poet, who disappeared in 1971 and who, according to Kingston, was one of the few people who wrote poems and also knew what a poem is. She admits that she keeps some of Welch's advice on writing within view of her desk.

The final essay in the collection, "A Sea Worry," concerns Kingston's son's passion for bodysurfing. She worries that he will become addicted to the experience: "I am afraid that the boys give themselves up to the ocean's mindlessness" (67). So, together with Earll, she goes with her son to witness the ocean's hold on him since he cannot find the words to describe the experience himself. Words also fail the other young men they meet at the beach, and Kingston takes heart from the mystery of the ocean's power.

Through the Black Curtain. Berkeley: Friends of the Bancroft Library/University of California, Berkeley, 1987.

This collection, published by the Friends of the Bancroft Library at the University of California, Berkeley, reprints excerpts from Kingston's

SURFING

"Even when the assignment is about something else, the students write about surfing. They try to describe what it is to be inside the wave as it curls over them, making a tube or 'chamber' or 'green room' or 'pipeline' or 'time warp.' They write about the silence, the peace, 'no hassles,' the feeling of being reborn as they shoot out the end. They've written about the voice of God, the 'commandments' they hear. In the margins, they draw the perfect wave. Their writing is full of clichés. 'The endless summer,' they say. 'Unreal.'"

Maxine Hong Kingston

From "A Sea Worry," in *Hawai'i One Summer* (Honolulu: University of Hawaii Press, 1998), p. 68.

Dust jacket for Kingston's 1989 novel

first two books; it also includes brief episodes from the manuscript of her then-unpublished novel, *Tripmaster Monkey*.

Tripmaster Monkey: His Fake Book. New York: Knopf, 1989.

Set in 1963, Kingston's first novel draws on her experiences as a student at the University of California, Berkeley. The first chapter, "Trippers and Askers," introduces the hero, Wittman Ah Sing, as he walks through Golden Gate Park in San Francisco to meet a friend for coffee. Wittman is a Chinese American poet and beatnik, a recent Berkeley graduate who is living in San Francisco. After meeting Nanci Lee, the most attractive girl in his graduating class, he is encouraged to tell her about his family, his background, and his thoughts. He invites her to see his apartment and is surprised that she accepts. On the way, they stop at a bookstore where Nanci, an actress, can look for audition pieces. She wants to avoid typecasting in one of the few Oriental stereotypes that appear in the theater. She explains that when she is told to remove her shoes for an audition, she knows she is being considered for the role of an oriental peasant: "You only need high heels for the part of the oriental prostitute" (24). Wittman sympathizes with Nanci's difficulty and confesses the mortification he suffered when his school broke with their tradition of giving the lead role in the senior play to the student who had performed best academically—Wittman—and instead gave him a special role as master of ceremonies for the evening. He promises to write a part for her in his play that will make the audience love her for what she is.

At his apartment Wittman, desperate to impress Nanci, selects one of his poems to read for her. But when he asks for her opinion, she likens his work to that of the black poet LeRoi Jones. He is disappointed both in her and in himself, jumping about the apartment, upsetting furniture, and imitating her words as spitefully as he can. As he does this he reveals to her his true nature: "I am really: the present-day U.S.A. incarnation of the King of the Monkeys" (33). His violent antics frighten Nanci, who does not know the right words to calm him, so she hurriedly leaves. As the chapter ends, the narrator intrudes to announce to the reader that the story concerns Chinese American characters. The characters with whom the reader has been identifying are not the Caucasians that usually appear in literary works but are literary creations that express what the narrator calls "a peculiar, colored, slanted p.o.v." (34).

The next chapter, "Linguists and Contenders," opens with Wittman continuing his writing throughout the night until he must change into "a working stiff on his way to his paying job" (44). He works in the toy department of a large department store, where he takes the opportunity to try to dissuade customers from buying war toys and guns. Down in the stockroom, where he is to find bicycles for display, Wittman finds instead an aging stock boy who was once designated a Yale Younger Poet and now lives in the world he has created for himself in the stockroom. As Wittman leaves to take the bicycles up to the shop floor, he promises this poet, as he has done for Nanci, a part in his play. He describes the play as "including everything that is being left out, and everybody who has no place" (52). He then attends a performance of a sort, a presentation by the Mattel corporation of their new line of toys. By the end of the chapter Wittman has lost patience with his employer and the customers

WITTMAN AH SING AS MONKEY

"After two thousand days of quest, which takes a hundred chapters to tell, and twenty-four acts, seven days to perform, Monkey and his friends, Tripitaka on the white horse, Piggy, and Mr. Sandman, arrive in the West. The Indians give them scrolls, which they load on the white horse. Partway home, Monkey, a suspicious fellow, unrolls the scrolls, and finds that they are blank scrolls. 'What's this? We've been cheated. Those pig-catchers gave us nothing. Let's demand an exchange.' So, he and his companions go back, and they get words, including the Heart Sutra. But the empty scrolls had been the right ones all along."

Maxine Hong Kingston

From *Tripmaster Monkey: His Fake Book* (New York: Knopf, 1989), p. 42.

alike and quits his job, though in carefully symbolic style. He takes an organ-grinder's monkey and a Barbie bride doll from their packaging and arranges them with Barbie "on her back with her arms and veil and legs and white dress raised, and the monkey on top of her. Her legs held it hopping in place and clapping her with its cymbals. Her eyes opened and shut as the monkey bumped away at her" (64–65). As a customer exclaims at this perverse sight, Wittman just walks away.

In "Twisters and Shouters" Wittman first kills some time by going to the movies to see *West Side Story;* he identifies with what he calls the "glitz" of the production, the gangs "a-crouching and a-leaping, fight-dancing through the city" (70). He then boards the Oakland-Berkeley bus and, to his dismay, a plain, ungainly Chinese girl carrying boxes and bundles of food sits next to him. As the girl, named Judy, insists on telling him about her life and asking about his, Wittman tries to pretend he is Japanese and not Chinese at all, but then he has to listen to her views about the differences between Japanese and Chinese boys. When the bus pulls up at his stop, he finds that Judy is headed for the same party he is going to attend. But he refuses to arrive with "Miss Refreshment Committee bringing salt fish and rice" (81), so he walks around the block before arriving at the party. Wittman's best friend and the host, Lance, throws theme parties, and this one is no exception: "There was always a plot to these parties; the fun was figuring out what the point was, and who got it and who didn't. Creative paranoia" (81). Wittman moves through the crowd, identifying each group and clique, until he finds a girl reciting poetry from the top of the stairs. This encounter transforms the party for him: once she has told him her name, he believes that she is in pursuit of him. This encounter lends him the moral courage to embark upon the next task he must perform: "Clear up some friendship karma" (115). Wittman confronts Lance with all the resentments he harbors against him; in return, Lance tells him the story of his life. Taña, the girl in pursuit of Wittman, catches up with him and, at the beginning of the next chapter, "The Winners of the Party," counts as one of these winners.

The winners—those who have stayed up all night and seen the party through to its conclusion—are Wittman, Taña, Lance and his wife, Sunny, Nanci, and Judy. Wittman entertains them by reciting the part of his play that he has just completed about the King of the Monkeys. He begins to assign roles to his friends: "Lance Kamiyama will be Liu Pei; Charles Bogard Shaw will be Chang Fei; Wittman will be Gwan Goong. Nanci Lee and the other women will be audience for the time being" (141). Taña and Wittman stroll through Oakland at dawn to her apartment, where she sets out what will be the terms of their relationship—to

Wittman's disappointment, since he was wondering how to raise that issue himself. They spend the day driving around San Francisco and visit the Coit Tower, where they encounter a friend of Taña's who has evaded the draft by becoming an ordained minister of the Universal Life Church. To assist Wittman in escaping the draft, Taña's friend not only ordains him but also, then and there, marries Wittman and Taña.

In the next chapter, "Ruby Long Legs' and Zeppelin's Song of the Open Road," Wittman and his new bride have a picnic at the Palace of Fine Arts, where he presents Taña with his wedding gift, a wedding story "from the tradition of the Heroic Couple on the Battlefield that will turn you into a Chinese," he warns her (172). They travel to Sacramento and visit Wittman's mother, Ruby Ah Sing, who is playing mah jong with her friends who, like her, have all been in show business. Wittman finds that his grandmother, PoPo—who may or may not be his grandmother; she appeared at his parents' door one day and they took her in—has gone camping with his father, Zeppelin Ah Sing. They go in search of her at his father's "river camp" (196). There, Zeppelin is playing poker with his friends, fishing poles staked at the water. He tells how he took PoPo to Reno so she could gamble and left her there; Taña and Wittman set off in search of her but are unable to find her. On the journey back Taña speculates about effective excuses for not going to work the next day, but Wittman cannot help her. He is beginning to feel oppressed by the obligations he has undertaken: "He had to create for Nanci Lee a theater. And find his PoPo. And keep Taña for richer, for poorer" (223).

The following chapter, "A Song for Occupations," relates Wittman's efforts to register as unemployed. He and Taña have devised a plan in which each of them will work for half the year and collect unemployment benefits during the other half. After registering, Wittman attends an interview with an employment counselor who must be convinced that the kind of job for which he is qualified is a position as a playwright. The narrator comments, "Wittman's not crazy and he's not lazy. The reason he doesn't have right livelihood is that our theater is dead" (249). Wittman approaches the Benevolent Association to produce a play in their hall, but he must tell a story to convince them that his play will be worth performing. He argues, "We make theater, we make community" (261). As he leaves, having gained permission to use the hall for his theater, he encounters PoPo on the street, and she tells him that she met someone and was married in Reno. After hearing her story, Wittman enlists her help with his play. When he telephones his mother to inform her about PoPo's whereabouts, he takes the opportunity to ask his mother to join in the play as well. He tells her, "I'm producing a show. I'm a show producer.

And our Joang Wah [the Benevolent Association] will sponsor. They like see you and the aunties do your historic War Bonds Rescue China act" (269). But Ruby objects that the war she helped to promote ended with the use of nuclear weapons. Then she was unthinking, but now when she thinks about war, she thinks about the prospect of Wittman's being drafted to fight in Vietnam. Her advice is that he should not produce a play but hurry to Canada instead.

In "A Pear Garden in the West," Wittman gathers his theatrical troupe: his mother and aunties, Lance and Sunny, Taña, Nanci Lee, and the stock boy from the department store. Everyone Wittman has encountered in the narrative comes to the theater, where he guides them through a rehearsal of his play. The narrator comments: "To entertain and educate the solitaries that make up a community; the play will be a combination revue-lecture" (288). The play is to be performed on Halloween, and the following chapter, "Bones and Jones," describes the opening night. Wittman stages the "War of the Three Kingdoms," which incorporates all the conventions of Chinese theater, all the racist stereotypes about Orientals, and all the prominent Chinese American writers of the earlier twentieth century. The play ends in a grand fireworks show that seems so real that fire engines arrive to douse the flames.

In the final chapter of the novel, "One-Man Show," the narrator remarks, "Our monkey, master of change, staged a fake war, which might very well be displacing a real war. Wittman was learning that one big bang-up show has to be followed up with a second show, a third show, shows until something takes hold. He was defining a community, which will meet every night for a season. Community is not built once-and-for-all; people have to imagine, practice, and re-create it" (306). Here, at the end of the narrative, Wittman is given his voice and allowed the space in which to express his thoughts and feelings about his play. He reveals his disappointment that reviewers have praised his work for being exotic, "eastern," and different; he is insulted that it is judged on "Chinese" terms and evaluated according to reviewers' stereotypical views of Chinese culture: "We've failed with our magnificence of explosions to bust through their Kipling. I'm having to give instruction. There is no East here. West is meeting West. This was all West. All you saw was West. This is The Journey In the West" (308). Wittman goes on to challenge these stereotypes and the racist practices to which they give rise: the cosmetic surgery Asian women undergo to make themselves look less oriental, the racist jokes about the sexuality of Asian men and women, and the movies that represent emasculated or evil images of Chinese men. "They have an enslavement wish for us, and they have a death wish, that we die" (319). Wittman suggests that Chinese actors sabotage the stereotypical roles they are asked to play by subverting the "Chinese shtick, make free to say whatever you want. True things. Pass messages, 'Eat shit, James Bond. Kiss my yellow ass'" (325). In his play he challenges the notion that Chinese do not express affection, and later he "unbrainwashes" (329) those who still believe this notion by asking everyone to kiss someone in the room. In this way Wittman fashions the loving community that it is his mission as an artist to create.

CRITICAL SUMMARY

The early critical response to Kingston's work was quite enthusiastic; reviewers were full of praise for *The Woman Warrior* and its then-unknown creator. Since that time, the mature response to her work has been rich and varied. Her writing has been interpreted in feminist, Chinese American, and postmodernist terms. Critics have used diverse contemporary theoretical perspectives to approach her works: the methods of narrative analysis proposed by Mikhail Bakhtin and the feminist concepts theorized by Hélène Cixous, for example.

Diane Simmons's study *Maxine Hong Kingston* (1999), published in the Twayne's United States Authors series, devotes three chapters to a lengthy account of *The Woman Warrior;* Simmons also discusses *China Men* and *Tripmaster Monkey.* The focus of her approach to Kingston's work is the theme of transcendence. Simmons analyzes the ways in which Kingston represents the desire to transcend fear and brutality through characters who confront racial and gender prejudices, yet retain their full humanity. Racism and sexism are linked in the books as mutually supportive systems of oppression. These systems place the oppressed and marginalized in a position of cultural invisibility, and Simmons uses a parallel with the work of the postcolonial critic Edward Said to illustrate her perception that Kingston focuses upon "the way in which the powerless are defined by the controlling narratives of the powerful. . . ."[1] This point leads Simmons to a consideration of the ways in which Kingston's characters set about the task of rewriting the oppressive historical and cultural narratives within which they have been situated and according to which they have been defined. This means that Chinese women dispute the ways in which they have been rendered powerless by traditional Chinese images of femininity; in the same way Chinese men dispute the Western, and specifically American, racial stereotypes that have "feminized" them and made them powerless.[2]

Simmons's discussion of *The Woman Warrior* addresses, within this critical context, the nature of the images of women represented by Kingston: the woman as outsider, the woman as savior, and the transformation of Mulan (the woman warrior of traditional myth) into a contemporary Chinese American. Simmons then turns to an analysis of Kingston's use of the shaman figure to examine the role of women in Chinese culture and in the challenge presented to this culture by "the forces of rebellion, Western economic imperialism, the chaos and banditry of warlordism, the suffering of Japanese occupation, and finally the dislocation of emigration, as experienced by Kingston's own emigrant parents and grandparents."[3] In the United States, a society in which ghosts appear to Chinese immigrants to dominate, the female shaman confronts the ghosts and attempts to hold the world together against the forces of chaos. This idea informs Simmons's account of the character of Brave Orchid, who is shown initially as the village shaman, later as a medical student, and finally as a doctor. Simmons reveals a parallel that Kingston develops between the figure of the woman warrior, who battles against the forces of physical chaos—bandits, evil barons, and the corrupt emperor—and Brave Orchid, who struggles against the ghosts that embody the forces of psychic chaos. As Simmons points out, Brave Orchid, like the woman warrior, prevails because she is strong and righteous. After finishing medical school, she returns to her village in triumph as a hero, to be embraced by the family she has left behind, and she struggles not simply to defeat her enemies but to establish a new order. This extended parallel between the two feminine figures enables Kingston to examine the ways in which women can transform their role within the patriarchal Confucian system. Both the woman warrior and Brave Orchid resist the role of the useless and parasitical woman, becoming instead heroes of their people. Simmons comments, "Women, as Kingston defines them, have the power to change the world. Ironically, their very power is a symptom of dislocation, the world gone wrong."[4] The mythical woman warrior is able to leave behind her aggressive warrior-self and return to the role of submissive wife and daughter, secure in the knowledge of her heroic past. But the shaman figure is more ambivalent, mistrusted and even feared for her relationship to the underworld. As Simmons perceives, the young Kingston in *The Woman Warrior* "expresses a similar distrust and fear. Understanding the mother's ability to "eat anything," to crush anything that stands in her way, and also, when necessary, to cut her losses—as a doctor she treats only those she can cure—the daughter wonders how a less-than-perfect girl like herself fits into her mother's economy of survival."

Kingston's representation of women includes not only the heroes, however: she also depicts the victims of the male-dominated Confucian social system. These victims include Kingston's No Name Aunt and Brave Orchid's sister, Moon Orchid. Of course, Brave Orchid herself is not an entirely heroic character, and Kingston represents quite starkly the fierce determination that she must sustain without respite throughout her life and in her dealings with everyone, without exception. Brave Orchid banishes from her own behavior all those characteristics that are exemplified by her sister. Moon Orchid is, like the flower her name suggests, a delicate and beautiful yet useless woman who needs the protection offered by the patriarchal kinship system. According to Simmons, Kingston deliberately contrasts the two sisters in order to test the two models of femininity they represent. Brave Orchid struggles to be accepted as a woman by her family and society; Moon Orchid is the type of woman who is submissive, decorative, and pampered by the men around her. Simmons invokes the figure of Ch'ang-o, the Moon Goddess of Chinese myth, to explain Kingston's characterization of Moon Orchid. In Simmons's account the story of Ch'ang-o and her husband, the Divine Archer who lives in the sun, represents "'woman's eternal separation from her husband,' as well as her life as a reflection of her husband's light."[5] Moon Orchid was left behind in Hong Kong by her husband, prevented by immigration laws from accompanying him to the United States, and thus she has no part in his American life. The life that she has lived in Hong Kong, paid for by her absent husband, is one of pampered luxury, evidenced by the elegant clothes and expensive jewelry she is wearing when she finally arrives in California. But when Moon Orchid confronts her husband, he denies her the identity of the banished or abandoned wife, telling her that she is to him like a character in a book he read a long time ago. His denial of her relation to him undermines Moon Orchid's sense of reality. This denial also brings Brave Orchid face to face with the limits of her own power: she is unable to make this man appreciate the traditional social order that she is trying to restore. He has left behind the Chinese kinship and other social practices of his youth and has become entirely American. Brave Orchid cannot restore her sister to her traditional place as first wife; instead, she has brought her sister to a place where she is alienated from her accustomed cultural role. Moon Orchid gradually loses her mind and dies. As Simmons comments, "The bold actions that helped Brave Orchid continue to see herself as female avenger have destroyed Moon Orchid's self-image as a lovely, passive, pampered traditional Chinese wife, living in the reflected light of her husband."[6] In Kingston's world women must fight or they will not survive.

Simmons not only contrasts Brave Orchid with Moon Orchid; she also explains a parallel between the young Kingston and her aunt. Kingston fears that her own passivity and silence, her inability to reconcile Chinese and American concepts of femininity in her own person, will result in the loss of her sanity. She wants to be prized and protected but fears that this soft helplessness will be her downfall. She strives to be tough, bold, and aggressive like her mother. Just as her mother triumphed over the "Sitting Ghost" (69), who haunts a room in the medical college until Brave Orchid exorcises it, so Kingston must drive away the retarded boy with whom she fears her parents will arrange a marriage for her. But this action is not perceived by her mother as the driving away of a ghost; rather, Brave Orchid sees it as evidence that her daughter has embraced the ghost world and become herself a ghost. From this position of exile Kingston turns to the historical figure of Ts'ai Yen, a Chinese princess who was kidnapped by barbarians and created poetry from her experience of exile from two opposed worlds. Simmons gives a detailed account of Ts'ai Yen's poetic work and explains how the poetry chronicles her personal history of captivity and her eventual return home. Simmons argues, "With this, Kingston works her final transformation of the book, changing grief, loss, and subjugation into a new, bold beauty, a heroism that surpasses that of Kingston's other heroines."[7]

Simmons uses her interpretation of *The Woman Warrior* as the framework for her discussion of Kingston's two subsequent books, *China Men* and *Tripmaster Monkey*. Whereas in *The Woman Warrior* Kingston addresses the ways in which women are subjected to the sexist definitions of femininity that are part of patriarchal culture, in *China Men* she looks to the demeaning, racist images of Chinese masculinity that operate in America, and in *Tripmaster Monkey* she identifies the forces of consumerism and militarism that dictate the values and interests of all Americans—not only Chinese or Asian Americans. According to Simmons, in all of her work Kingston portrays the modern world as fundamentally broken and in need of repair. In *The Woman Warrior* the figure of the woman poet, Ts'ai Yen, is able to transform loss into beauty and cross-cultural alienation into cultural synthesis and harmony. The male characters of *China Men*—Kingston's father, her grandfathers, and her youngest brother—find themselves in exile from China and under assault by the daily racism they encounter in America. Kingston tells their stories in order to reveal the heroism of their lives and to demonstrate the heroic effort they have made to retain their humanity despite the brutalizing effects of racism. Her father she likens to the exiled poet-scholar Ch'ü Yüan, who sought transcendence from a corrupt world. She depicts her grandfathers—one who labored on a Hawaiian sugar plantation, the other on the construction of the transcontinental railroad—as heroic pioneers of the American nation. Her brother Kingston represents in the same way she has depicted the abducted princess Ts'ai Yen in *The Woman Warrior*. Simmons observes that these characters engage with the conflicting pressures of cultural duality; they negotiate the opposing demands of home and the place of exile, of self and other. Kingston's brother has to negotiate the complex issues raised by the Vietnam War and his role in the military conflict as an American serviceman of Asian descent. Like Ts'ai Yen, he is able to form a sense of personal integrity by synthesizing different aspects (Asian and American) of his sense of self with his historical experiences; he is able to join satisfactorily his personal ethics with the cultural demands made upon him.

The sexual discrimination to which women are subject offers a parallel with the racial discrimination to which Chinese American men are subject. Simmons broaches the issue of how these themes are twinned in *China Men* by explaining Kingston's use of the nineteenth-century Chinese novel *Flowers in the Mirror* (1828), by Li Ju-chen. The novel tells of the adventures of the merchant Lin and his brother-in-law, Tang Ao. Kingston retells the story of the capture of Lin by a society of women who use him as a sexual object, but she substitutes for the merchant the scholar Tang Ao, who calls to mind Kingston's portrait of her father as a scholar in exile. She opens *China Men* with this story, and Simmons argues that "By focusing on sexual oppression and hinting at the connection between the man who is forcibly feminized and the men who came to the United States, Kingston suggests that the oppression of women by Chinese patriarchalism and the oppression of Chinese men in a racist America feel the same, indeed, are the same."[8] The feminization of the powerless by the powerful is characteristic of the stereotypes created by a fundamentally oppressive and exploitative culture. Kingston takes these figures out of this oppressive context and rewrites their lives and identities in terms of mythical Chinese heroes and American founding fathers. This transformation of identity Simmons traces as Kingston's primary effort in her depiction of Chinese and Chinese American women under patriarchy and immigrant Chinese men in a racist and xenophobic America. Both *The Woman Warrior* and *China Men* conclude with a portrait of a character who is able to negotiate the complex demands made by Chinese and American cultures.

Simmons argues that Wittman Ah Sing in *Tripmaster Monkey* accepts himself as both American and Chinese and refuses to be torn by the differences he harbors in himself. He does not simply represent the synthesis of difference, he is also an agent of synthesis, in Simmons's view. She asserts that through the character of Wittman, Kingston sets out not only to "transform the identities of Chinese Americans, but to transform the identity of America itself, to integrate Chinese mythology, the Chinese experience, and Wittman's own personal experience into the imagination of his audience."[9] What Wittman seeks to shift American cultural identity away from is a destructive identification with the forces of consumerism and militarism. He operates in the political environment of Berkeley in the early 1960s, at the dawn of the hippie drug culture, when the military conflict in southeast Asia was beginning to generate domestic opposition. He opposes a vision of "mainstream Americans [as] increasingly trained to identify themselves in terms of their relationship to corporate and military culture [where] their authentic selves have been rendered invisible, both to themselves and to each other."[10] Simmons reveals the parallel relationships among what she calls "the dehumanizing forces of racism," the "isolating soul-death of consumerism," and the "dehumanizing energies of militarism" in Kingston's novel.[11] Wittman uses powerful images of community, heroism, and loyalty to combat the forces of dehumanization and alienation. Kingston presents these images by using traditional Chinese stories and myths, especially the stories of the trickster Monkey, the hero of Wu Ch'eng-en's *Journey to the West* (1592) and the third-century Chinese story of the Three Kingdoms. Simmons gives a detailed account of Kingston's use of these sources.

Simmons includes in her study a substantial biographical essay which gives an account of the characteristic themes of Kingston's work and the psychological influences in her early life that have had an impact upon her writing. Simmons also considers the impact on Kingston's work of the politicized atmosphere at Berkeley during her time there as a student. Simmons discusses Kingston's status as a Chinese American writer and the attacks made upon her by Chinese American male critics such as Frank Chin; she also considers Kingston's visit to China in 1984 and the reception of her work in China. In addition, Simmons explores the relationships Kingston forged with each of her parents, who feature so prominently in her first two books. Simmons's short 1997 interview with Kingston covers such topics as a work-in-progress, "The Fifth Book of Peace," the relationship between Western individualism and Confucianism, and the role of the woman writer in contemporary American culture.

Conversations with Maxine Hong Kingston (1998), edited by Paul Skenazy and Tera Martin, brings together a selection of published interviews with Kingston, prefaced with a chronology of events in her life and an introduction by the editors. The most common topic that recurs throughout these interviews is that of writing: how Kingston goes about it, what her views are about its importance, and the means by which she has transformed her experiences into literature. These experiences of cultural duality, sexism, racism, and the transcendence of suffering and oppression, are also discussed in detail throughout the book. The collection represents a chronological range of interviews; the earliest is one conducted by Gary Kubota that was first published in the *Hawaii Observer* in 1977; other newspaper pieces include Timothy Pfaff's 1980 interview, first published in *The New York Times Book Review*. The latest of the interviews, conducted by Eric Schroeder, was published in the spring 1996 issue of *Writing from the Edge*. The collection provides valuable background information about the creation of each of Kingston's books.

The Woman Warrior dominates much of the published criticism on Kingston. Sau-ling Cynthia Wong has collected a selection of important essays on the book in *Maxine Hong Kingston's The Woman Warrior: A Casebook* (1999). This collection provides a representative sampling of the body of critical work that has developed around the text, the most important approaches to it that have been adopted, and the primary issues raised by critical interpretations of the book. Wong proceeds from the assumption that "by the late 1990s *The Woman Warrior* has become deeply embedded in American feminist and 'multicultural' critical and pedagogical practices."[12] Wong's selection of essays covers the controversies that have surrounded *The Woman Warrior*: criticism of Kingston's use of traditional Chinese myths and stories, reactions to her work by Chinese American male writers, and the place occupied by her style of writing within the Asian American literary canon.

Shirley Geok-lin Lim has collected essays on *The Woman Warrior* with a pedagogical emphasis in *Approaches to Teaching Kingston's The Woman Warrior* (1991). The first part of the book lists "materials" such as editions of the book, Kingston's other works, background studies, and critical studies. The second part includes a personal statement by Kingston and essays on the cultural and historical contexts of the book, as well as pedagogical contexts and critical contexts within which the text can be placed. The essays cover such issues as Kingston's use of traditional Chinese stories, the Asian literary background of *The Woman Warrior*, and the text in relation to Asian American historiography. Pedagogical contexts discussed include student responses to *The Woman Warrior* and the teaching of the book in women's studies, history, and composition courses, as well as in settings such as community colleges and military academies. Dominant themes of the book that are highlighted for discussion include the search for identity, the imagery of ghosts, storytelling and truth-telling, and autobiography. Contributors also consider the issue of genre in relation to *The Woman Warrior,* for example in "Engendering Genre: Gender and Nationalism in *China Men* and *The Woman Warrior,*" by Leilani Nishimi.

Useful and interesting essays on Kingston and her cultural background also appear in general studies on Asian American writing. *An Interethnic Companion to Asian American Literature* (1997), edited by King-Kok Cheung, includes an account by Sau-ling Cynthia Wong of Chinese American literature that provides a background to Kingston's work. The volume also features Lim's discussion of immigration and diaspora, both prominent themes in Kingston's writing, in a survey of Asian American writing. *Reading the Literatures of Asian America* (1992), edited by Lim and Amy Ling, includes Cheung's essay "'Don't Tell': Imposed Silences in *The Color Purple* and *The Woman Warrior,*" Patricia Lin's essay "Clashing Constructs of Reality: Reading Maxine Hong Kingston's *Tripmaster Monkey* as Indigenous Ethnography," and Sau-ling Cynthia Wong's essay "Ethnicizing Gender: An Exploration of Sexuality as Sign in Chinese Immigrant Literature." Ling's study *Between Worlds: Women Writers of Chinese Ancestry* (1990) discusses both *The Woman Warrior* and *China Men* and usefully places Kingston's work within the tradition of Chinese women's writing in English. In a 1995 essay, "Maxine Hong Kingston and the Dialogic Dilemma of Asian American Writers," Ling addresses the relationship between ethnography, psychoanalysis, and literature in the work of Asian American writers generally and that of Kingston in particular.

ART IMITATING LIFE

There are clear parallels between Kingston's literary works and her life, most obviously in the autobiographical elements of *The Woman Warrior* (the subtitle of which identifies it as a memoir) and *China Men.* She does not even change the names of the characters in these texts; for example, her mother is called by her actual name, Brave Orchid. Family history, cultural mythology, and factual history provide the materials for these books. The settings Kingston uses are the village in China described in her mother's stories and the city of Stockton, in which she grew up. She has said that an important part of her determination to be a writer is the need to discover what Stockton is and how she relates to the place that formed her: "I think that there is a lot in Stockton that is anti-beauty, anti-intellectual, even anti-life. All my life, I've lived in and around Skid Row in Stockton. I say all my life because even when I went away to school or I went to live in Hawaii, I always came back to Stockton because that's where my parents are and my roots and my brothers and sisters, and my Chinatown."[13] In this way, Kingston reasons, Stockton is a good place for a writer to grow up because many of the large issues that must be confronted in literature are confronted every day by the people who live there: how to foster social responsibility, how to make beauty out of the ugly and tawdry, how to make sense out of what seems senseless, and how to construct a community out of a gathering of "stoned people, hoboes, dealers, and criminals," as she has described the human landscape of the city.[14] But the ability to recognize the stories with which she is surrounded and to know their significance is an important aspect of Kingston's maturity as a writer. She has no interest in creating an attractive, exotic image of the Chinese community in Stockton or imposing upon that community a stereotypical image derived from San Francisco's famous Chinatown.

There are autobiographical parallels in *Tripmaster Monkey* with Kingston's Berkeley years. For example, the party scene in which Wittman's future wife, Taña, reads her poetry aloud is reminiscent of the writer's own experience of such parties in Berkeley in the 1960s. She recalls, "You'd go to a party, and what I'd love about the party is that the poets would get up and read, would entertain one another with poetry."[15] In a 1983 interview Kingston discusses the writing of this scene to illustrate the relationship between her life and her fiction, describing how she transforms the events of her life to make them sufficiently interesting: "I'm writing a party scene that takes one Saturday night, but in this party I've used the fifty most interesting parties I've been to in twenty years. All of that amounts to just one good party."[16] In the same interview Kingston addresses the difficulty of writing fiction that is set in a recognizably real world. As an example she cites the assassination of President John F. Kennedy, which happened in the year in which *Tripmaster Monkey* is set, 1963. She asks, "if I'm writing a novel, do I have the right to ignore the Kennedy assassination? May I have my characters go right through November and into Christmas and not even notice that assassination because I don't care to write about it? Because it's not interesting to me? I think that's a problem."[17] Kingston poses no solution to this difficult problem of the relationship between historical reality and the world of her fiction.

At the end of *Tripmaster Monkey* Kingston includes a list of all the friends who have contributed in some way to the story and an indication of what they have contributed. For example, she thanks Britt Pyland "for his arrangements of postcards at the airport" (341), something Wittman's friend Lance does in the novel. She explains the list as "more than just an acknowledgement; it's the admission that we're part of something, that when we're alone writing we're not alone—that the imaginative life and the real life intertwine."[18] Another point at which the imaginative and the real intersect in the novel is Wittman's outrage at being treated as if he does not belong, as if he is not an American, which expresses much of Kingston's anger about the exclusion of the Chinese from official American history and culture. Seen from this angle, Kingston's writing is essentially about confronting the fact of exclusion and exposing the false assumptions that have obscured the contribution made by Chinese Americans to the development of the United States.

KINGSTON'S WORK IN HISTORY

The Woman Warrior is widely acknowledged as a literary masterpiece and is among the most frequently taught contemporary American literary texts. Kingston was awarded some of the most prestigious prizes for which the book was qualified to compete, an achievement that she repeated with *China Men*. With these works she redefined the possibilities for autobiographical writing in the late twentieth century. *Tripmaster Monkey* has been acclaimed as an important example of postmodernist fiction, comparable with Thomas Pynchon's *Gravity's Rainbow* (1973) and William S. Burroughs's *Naked Lunch* (1959). In the introduction to their collection of Kingston's interviews, Skenazy and Martin comment, "It is estimated that her work is the most anthologized of any living American writer, and that she is read by more American college students than any other living author. Students, particularly Asian American women, look to her as a model, find themselves in her tales, seek her out with sycophantic regularity. She has opened the way to a whole generation of Asian American writers who have found a national audience for the first time."[19]

Kingston has the reputation of being one of the most innovative of contemporary Chinese American writers. She is the most prominent Asian American author of her generation, and she leads the renaissance of Asian American women's writing that began in the late 1970s. Kingston's work coincides historically with the emergence of feminist criticism as perhaps the most influential development in the contemporary academic world. A lasting impact of the Civil Rights movement of the

1960s upon literary study has been the prominence accorded to writers from ethnic groups, such as Asian American writers. Kingston herself perceives that her work is part of a larger movement in American literature: "Amy Tan published *The Joy Luck Club,* and Hisaye Yamamoto published *Seventeen Syllables;* Frank Chin has a collection of short stories, and I think maybe Ruth-Anne Lumm McKunn just came out with her book on Chinese families. Jessica Hagedorn's in the spring, and Bharati Mukherjee's is in the fall. She won the National Book Critics Circle Award. Something great must be going on."[20] She agrees that her work has helped to inspire this flowering of creativity.

Kingston's status as a feminist and as a Chinese American opens her work to current political styles of literary interpretation, and this has contributed to the popularity of her books in college and university curricula. Only time will judge the enduring appeal of her work, but there is reason to believe that she may prove to be one of the most influential and important writers of her generation.

ADAPTATIONS

Kingston's work has been translated in China, Hong Kong, and Taiwan in both legal editions and pirated editions, which she has described as quite badly translated. In the People's Republic of China, the Language Institute translated *The Woman Warrior* and *China Men* into the national standard language as well as into Cantonese. Kingston estimates that some twenty translations have been made of *The Woman Warrior.*[21]

Kingston reports that she has had offers to adapt *The Woman Warrior* as a motion picture, but she has postponed making a decision because she feels she knows little about the movie business: "One thing I do know, however, is that I don't want any haoles with taped eyelids playing roles as Chinese."[22] Though she admits to having reservations about possible adaptations of *The Woman Warrior* into a movie, Kingston was quite pleased with a 1994 stage adaptation performed by the Berkeley Repertory Theater and was closely involved in the dramatization of the book and the production. She did not write the script herself; rather, the playwright was Deborah Rogin, but Kingston was pleased with the adaptation of the narrative into dramatic form: "Her [Rogin's] feat was to find an organizing principle for my complex, non-linear books. She has braided three strands together—myth, ancestral history, and the life of a young girl." Kingston continues, "I am amazed at the richness and beauty of the play—the costumes hand sewn in

杜鵑休向耳邊啼

MAXINE HONG KINGSTON 原著·張時譯

Cover of a Chinese translation of *China Men*
published in Hong Kong

China, the immense stage sets and glorious lights by Ming Cho Lee, the voices of the actors transmitting my stories mouth-to-ear, the fusion of Western and Chinese music, the kung fu acrobatics. Much of what I write came out of talk-story. I put talk-story into text. Now, the play returns text to talk-story, and children and non-readers can appreciate these myths and legends too."[23]

The casting of the roles presented particular problems, in that while there was no shortage of actresses who could play the delicate and feminine Moon Orchid, or indeed any of the "failed women," as Kingston refers to them, it was difficult to find an actress to play Brave Orchid, leading her to remark, "I think this shows that in 1986 the feminine, bound-foot, dainty type is with us. But where is the peasant woman with the big feet who is fierce and strong and of the earth, and yet beautiful?"[24] (She had held workshops in 1986 with a view to developing a play based on the book.) The casting, however, was a triumph of what Kingston sees as nontraditional casting. She speculates, "a movie would try to make everybody look the same, like everybody in the family would have to look the same. But in the play, it was really wonderful to have Vietnamese accents, Japanese American accents, Hawaiian accents, a Singaporean accent, and all the different Chinese accents."[25]

PUBLIC RESPONSE

In 1979 *Time* magazine named *The Woman Warrior* one of the top ten nonfiction works of the 1970s, and ten years later the book was still listed as a best-seller on the trade-paperback lists.[26] In the introduction to *Maxine Hong Kingston's The Woman Warrior: A Casebook,* Sau-ling Cynthia Wong calls the book "one of the most widely circulated and frequently taught literary texts by a living American author."[27] Kingston is aware of the extent of her popularity, remarking that on college campuses young women refer to *The Woman Warrior* simply as "the book," which they carry with them like a badge or talisman.[28] She has been honored with literary prizes and honorary academic degrees, but she is also quite popular with nonacademic readers. She has a large readership in China, noting proudly that there she is perceived to be part of Chinese literary tradition. In an interview with Marilyn Chin and again in a forum when she was asked about her Chinese readership, Kingston explained: "I have a place in the 'canon' of Chinese literature. I learned this when I visited China. They consider me 'one of them.' My name in China is Hong Ting Ting. They feel that they cut off all their roots during the Cultural Revolution; they got rid of everything, their roots to the past and their roots into the future (in fact they try to write something they call 'roots' literature). They see me as one who was put in a very privileged position and continued writing on 'roots,' and they feel that I saved some of their roots for them."[29]

NOTES

1.   Diane Simmons, *Maxine Hong Kingston* (New York: Twayne, 1999), p. 51.

2.   Ibid., p. 52.

3.   Ibid., p. 73.

4.   Ibid., p. 81.

5.   Ibid., p. 85.

6.   Ibid., p. 91.

7.   Ibid., p. 105.

8.   Ibid., p. 109.

9.   Ibid., p. 141.

10. Ibid.,

11. Ibid.

12. Sau-ling Cynthia Wong, *Maxine Hong Kingston's The Woman Warrior: A Casebook* (New York & Oxford: Oxford University Press, 1999), pp. 4–5.

13. Paul Skenazy, "Coming Home," in *Conversations with Maxine Hong Kingston,* edited by Skenazy and Tera Martin (Jackson: University Press of Mississippi, 1998), p. 114.

14. **Ibid.**

15. Shelley Fisher Fishkin, "Interview with Maxine Hong Kingston," in *Conversations with Maxine Hong Kingston,* p. 166.

16. Phyllis Hoge Thompson, "This is the Story I Heard: A Conversation with Maxine Hong Kingston and Earll Kingston," *Biography,* 6, no. 1 (1983): 7.

17. Ibid., p. 2.

18. Skenazy, "Coming Home," p. 110.

19. Skenazy and Martin, introduction to *Conversations with Maxine Hong Kingston,* p. **vii**.

20. Marilyn Chin, "Writing the Other: A Conversation with Maxine Hong Kingston," in *Conversations with Maxine Hong Kingston*, p. 98.

21. Wong, introduction to *Maxine Hong Kingston's The Woman Warrior: A Casebook*, p. 12.

22. Gary Kubota, "Maxine Hong Kingston: Something Comes from Outside Onto the Paper," in *Conversations with Maxine Hong Kingston*, p. 4.

23. Neila C. Seshachari, "Reinventing Peace: Conversations with Tripmaster Maxine Hong Kingston," in *Conversations with Maxine Hong Kingston*, p. 214.

24. Jody Hoy, "To Be Able to See the Tao," in *Conversations with Maxine Hong Kingston*, p. 48.

25. Eric J. Schroeder, "As Truthful as Possible: An Interview with Maxine Hong Kingston," in *Conversations with Maxine Hong Kingston*, p. 224.

26. Skenazy and Martin, introduction to *Conversations with Maxine Hong Kingston*, p. xxiv.

27. Wong, introduction to *Maxine Hong Kingston's The Woman Warrior: A Casebook*, p. 3.

28. Maxine Hong Kingston, "Personal Statement," in *Approaches to Teaching Kingston's The Woman Warrior*, edited by Shirley Geok-lin Lim (New York: Modern Language Association, 1991), p. 24.

29. Fishkin, "Interview with Maxine Hong Kingston," p. 166.

KINGSTON ON KINGSTON

As a child Kingston found the essay form difficult to learn because she was more interested in imaginative creation than in logical argument. But the publication of her essay "Literature in a Scientific Age: Lorenz' *King Solomon's Ring*" in *English Journal* in 1973 helped to convince her that she could think and present her ideas rationally in the disciplined form of the academic essay. Since then Kingston has written many essays and contributed to academic publications, such as the Modern Language Association's 1991 volume *Approaches to Teaching Kingston's The Woman Warrior.*

KINGSTON ON FEMINISM

I think to be a good feminist first you realize who you are yourself as a woman and, when you become a strong woman, then you face the Other. Whatever the Other is, whether it's men, the rest of the world, people of other races—whatever to you, in your psyche, the Other is. And so, when you become a strong woman, you also face the yang, and so, of course the next book has to be about men, that's the other half of the universe. So to me it's profoundly feminist to write about men, to be able to create men characters, and to understand what I previously could not understand.[1]

What comes to my mind is that there is actually a saving and nurturing force in the universe, and it is embodied in Kuan Yin, for example. These are names for that saving force and Kuan Yin is sometimes seen as a woman, sometimes as a man. She has many masculine incarnations in India, and she can be embodied in human imagination in these mythic figures. I think that it is easy for women to incorporate that force, and this is because women actually create life. We have babies; we actually hold a human being inside of ourselves, both in birth and in sex, and so I think that women's bodies are very naturally able to hold this force of salvation.[2]

At the end of the Chinese traditional chants, the Woman Warrior comes home and turns from a man, a general in armor, back into a beautiful woman, and then she presents herself to her army as a beautiful woman and sends the soldiers on their way. Now I had left that scene out of my version of *The Woman Warrior* because I was writing in 1975. I wanted a feminist book and I didn't understand the importance or why, in the ancient myth, you would have this strong figure turn into such a femi-

103

Kingston at the Vietnam Veterans Memorial, Washington, D.C. In 1992 she instituted a series of writing workshops for veterans of the Vietnam War and other wars.

nine person with make-up. The chant tells about her beautiful, long, black hair and how she wears it up and she puts flowers in it. She wears a silk dress and she's a classically beautiful woman. I left that out because I didn't see the need for a modern feminist to wear make-up. . . .

I want it very much now to be a hopeful story about homecoming from war, one that shows how a war veteran can transform herself into a peaceful, nurturing, mothering, feminine human being. She becomes more human and humane. . . .

Also, I am telling her story in a different context now, and I am writing about a different phase of human life. *The Woman Warrior* is still a story of adolescent growth. It tells the journey from being a girl to a woman and so there's just that rite of passage of a young person. But the way I want to use that story now is, I am writing about middle age, the middle of life and even the end of life. I'm talking about the end of a war. And here is not a knight setting out for adventure at the beginning of a *bildungsroman* but one who has finished the war. It is a story of how to come home, how to reintegrate oneself into one's family and community.[3]

KINGSTON ON WAR AND PEACE

The whole question of war and peace begins in *The Woman Warrior* [as Kingston's young protagonist deals with fears associated with World War II]. That little child is really worried. There's bombs going off. What war is this? How come is this [war] called World War Two? Was there a One? Will there be a Three? What's going on here? And I write about the trauma of seeing my first movie, which was a war movie. I'm wasting all my wishes on war. And so I see that I have had the same concerns from the very start and I'm bringing them more and more into mature thinking.[4]

I ended *China Men* when the brother returns from Vietnam. It ends on a very flat sentence, "OK, everything is OK." He did not kill anyone, and he was not killed. It's not triumphant, it's not heroic, it's just survival, and that was all the wisdom I knew. And now, 20 years later—I feel that 20 years is a period of time when we live through traumas, troubles come inside of us, and we process them, we live with them, we study them with the conscious mind, then we are able to put them into artistic expression. So 20 years later, my brothers have made lives for themselves beyond the war. They have come home, and they have been able to create peaceful, humane lives. And so, I need to continue "The Brother in Vietnam" past the adventure story and past the adolescent-young-man story into middle age. . . .

See again, *Tripmaster Monkey* ends during Wittman's late adolescence. Wittman is a boyish person and he has just gotten married but here's no commitment or understanding of what marriage is. Not enough time has gone by to test the marriage, to test the carrying out of one's values and principles. The story ends when he decides that he will be a draft evader. You know, for young people these are instant decisions. But the real test of a human being is a long term carrying out of ideas, and so the next book is about Wittman becoming older and middle-aged. . . .

It seems to me, like most of my ideas, [the work with veterans] came gradually. There is of course the Vietnam War and my own peace activism at that time. Also my having two brothers in the service during the Vietnam War. During that time, like other Peace Activists, I tried to think of ways to help stop the war, to help pacify all of us. I had many adventures at that time. We were in Hawaii. We were some of the people who held a church sanctuary for AWOL soldiers. All during the Vietnam War,

I could feel there was a darkness hanging over the whole world and it lasted for so long. I had a son and I was horrified that some day he would be drafted. All of these feelings of being a mother were very strong in me, and I felt very protective of not just my son but my brothers. And I didn't want my son to grow up in a world where there is going to be a draft. Those times were very interesting. People were trying to solve the most terrible problems. I have friends who also had children at that time and some of them had the baby at home without a doctor, thinking that maybe they won't register this baby. And if they don't register him, then he will never be drafted. And then the war ended so inconclusively. I was just looking through news clippings that I have of that period and soldiers were still trickling home in the mid-Seventies from Vietnam. So it was inconclusive—it wasn't an ending. And I was thinking, I want to make an ending. I want to be able to manipulate reality as easily as I can manipulate fiction. Do we imagine the world? If we imagine characters, can we cause them to appear in the real world? What if I could strongly write peace, I can cause an end to war. . . .

I was thinking, the end to the Vietnam War is not just that they stop shooting and we stop shooting. That's not the end. The end has to be something very wonderful. The Vietnamese have a commune in France. Thich Nhat Hanh, a Vietnamese monk, has a religious commune in France, and I was thinking how wonderful if I can bring a group of Vietnam veterans to live in community with Vietnamese people. . . .

I want to raise the money to take a group and go there and then I can just witness the coming together of all these people. To me, that would be a true ending to the war with Vietnam.[5]

KINGSTON ON HER PERSONAL PHILOSOPHY

I guess my sense of social responsibility comes from all my life, as far back as I can remember, my parents telling me those stories of the man with the writing on his back and of the woman warrior going into battle for her father. So I was raised with those stories. I think those stories passed on social responsibility to the children and to the young writer.

I think I've made readjustments and realignments so we can see things correctly. Like Confucianism has . . . a bad rap against it when we look at it in a certain feminist way, and also people who are Confucians will use the basic ideas [of Confucian philosophy] and put women down, and say "Oh little sister doesn't belong here. She has to be under the thumb of somebody else." What I've done is let us really look at the main point of Confucianism, which is that everybody has an honorable right place in society and it doesn't mean that little sister has to be crushed. It means she has a place. And she has power in that place and from her place she can influence the whole structure.[6]

The way I don't do it [teach writing] is the way Mrs. Garner taught us in the fourth grade. Mrs. Garner was an organized woman, who brought out a box of decorations for each holiday and new season. Year after year, she put up the same bulletin boards and gave the same lessons; we knew exactly what the younger brother or sister was learning and what would come next. Nowadays we teachers invent new courses each semester—The American Novel in Film, Science Fiction, The Alienated Adolescent, Lovers at War, etc. We never get to establish a file of tried and true ditto sheets like Mrs. Garner's. She pressed hers on a gelatin plate, and pulled duplicates one by one.

It was her tradition to have us make a notebook entitled *Gems*. She did not explain what "gems" were. The only other time we used that word was in "Columbia, the Gem of the Ocean," one of her favorite songs. The notebook was not about jewels, nor is "Columbia, the Gem of the Ocean." She let us pick out our own construction paper for the cover; I chose a pink nubby oatmeal paper, and lettered "Gems" in lime green. While we were numbering the pages the way she showed us, she stuck chalk into the fingers of the wood-and-wire rakelike thing that enabled her to draw five straight lines at one stroke. She usually made musical scales with it, but for "gems," she ran it back and forth until the blackboard looked like a sheet of binder paper. Then she wrote a "gem," which we were to copy word for word and line for line, indenting and breaking the lines the way she did. Perhaps the "gems" were a penmanship lesson, I thought, but wasn't that when we drew loops and zig-zags? Copying the "gems" was like art period, when she drew an apple on the board with red chalk, then a brown stem with a green leaf shooting off to the right. We copied this apple as exactly as we could, and she corrected our shapes with her art pencil. She had a drawer filled with the comic books she confiscated, another drawer of water pistols and another of slingshots. If I were to use her methods today, the students would beat me up. (I once confiscated some nunchakus, a pair of night sticks on a chain, which I put in my desk drawer.)

And yet it was in Mrs. Garner's classroom that I discovered that I could write poems. I remember the very moment the room filled with a light that would have been white except that the warm light off the wooden desks (with the inkwell holes and the pencil grooves) suffused it with yellow—and out of the air and into my head and down my arm and out my fingers ten, twenty verses in an a-b-b-a rhyme. The poem was about flying; I flew. . . .

One of my students who is now a published poet, Jody Manabe, said that she quit writing for one year because her seventh-grade teacher, a man, told her, "You write like a man."

The best I ever wrote in high school was when the teachers said, "Write whatever you like." Now I can appreciate what a daring assignment that is. I would not like to be caught saying that when an administrator or department head walks in to see if I have lesson plans.

The worst writing happened during the four years of college, which I attended when the English departments were doing the New Criticism (and the art department, Abstract Expressionism). The rule at our school was that an undergraduate could take one creative writing class, and she had to wait until junior or senior year. Poems, short stories, plays, and novels were what great masters wrote and what we students wrote about. We wrote essays.

The school system is dominated by the essay. And for me, essays would not become poems or stories. The real writing got stalled until after homework and graduation. The only place I could be fanciful was in the title. The professors wrote, "Purple prose," next to the few interesting phrases I could squeeze into "the body." Looking back on it, I believe the essay form was what drove English majors into becoming the most vituperative demonstrators during the student strikes.

My favorite method for teaching writing is to have the student write any old way. I tell them "I grade by quantity and not quality." By writing a hundred pages per semester, they have to improve—and the writing will find its form.

I tell the students that form—the epic, the novel, drama, the various forms of poetry—is organic to the human body. Petrarch did not invent the sonnet. Human heartbeat and language and voice and breath produce these rhythms. The teacher can look at a student's jumble of words and say, "I see you are moving toward the short story," or whatever. This is a good way to criticize and compliment—tell the young writer how close he or she is getting to which form.

To begin with form would probably work, too, as long as it's not the essay. Put a problem into a sonnet and it will help you state the problem, explore it, and solve it elegantly in a couplet. Ballads come naturally to students, who are lyric, and young like Keats and Shelley.

In *The Catcher in the Rye,* Holden takes an Oral Expression class where the students have to give spontaneous speeches, and whenever a speaker digresses, the class and Mr. Vinson yell, "Digression!" Sometimes a speaker can hardly talk anymore and gets an F. Mr. Vinson doesn't know that if you let somebody digress long enough, what he says will eventually take shape, a classical shape.

As a teacher, I have a stake in controlling that classroom, too. And the essay is orderly, easy to write and easy to grade; a computer can do it. Just check the thesis statement and make sure that each major paragraph backs up the thesis with arguments, examples, and quotes.

I do teach the essay—the three-paragraph essay, then the five-paragraph essay, then the term paper—so that my students can survive college. I try to throw in enough other kinds of writing to put the essay in perspective. When the class is over, though, kids probably forget everything but the essay. It is a form that the brain grasps. But if I become paralyzed worrying about the kid writers I am damaging, I try to remember how tough writers are. Kwan Kung, the god of war and literature, rides before us.[7]

I must write in a way that makes readers care about the people I create on paper. No matter that critics question what my genre is—fiction? nonfiction?—there is a reader in every audience who will ask: "How's your mother doing?"

My mother is fine, thank you, though she has high blood pressure and ought to be taking her prescription pills rather than the latest Chinatown remedy—honey and lemons just now, because specific herbs have not been available since June 4, 1989. She worries too much, and talks-story about the drug dealers on the block and their blatant m.o.'s. I advise her to pretend she doesn't notice. Should I tell her my idea? Put the pyramids of food and fruit and the shot glasses of Seagram's V.O. outside the gate. On the other hand, you aren't supposed to feed the bears at Yosemite; you call attention to yourself, and they don't understand when you run out of largesse.

Readers also ask how she feels about my writing. Well, since she doesn't read English, she can't get the fullest impact and power of my work. She reads the translations that have been pirated in Taiwan, Hong Kong, and China. Since pirates work fast, they use ready-made literary forms. They do not take the care to experiment with language or to try new shapes—to find the new shapes that I'm working in. The easiest given form is soap opera, which fakes passion and revelation. I suppose my mother thinks I am strong on plot and very entertaining, like her favorite American book, *Gone with the Wind.* She takes the world's praise of my work at face value and assumes she and our family come off well.

My father's reactions to my work have been more satisfying. I directly challenge him in *China Men:* "You'll just have to speak up with the real stories if I've got you wrong." The Hong Kong pirated edition of *China Men* has nice wide margins, in which my father wrote commentary in his beautiful calligraphic hand. Commentary is a poetic and religious tradition, writers answering one another in verse, furthering and finishing rhymes and ideas. Confucius wrote commentary on the *I Ching.* I donated that copy of *China Men* to the Bancroft Library. I took my father there to show him his words on display. He said in English to the people around him, "My writing."

To best appreciate *The Woman Warrior,* you do need to read *China Men.* You'll see that "I" achieve an adult narrator's voice. And you'll find out what else the people do. Brave Orchid comes to New York and takes up the role of wife. The feminist narrator journeys to the Land of Men. She finds the ancestors and sympathetically follows the brothers to Vietnam. "I" am nothing but who "I" am in relation to other people. In *The Woman Warrior* "I" begin the quest for self by understanding the archetypal mother. In *China Men,* "I" become more whole because of the ability to appreciate the other gender.

Young women on campuses carry *The Norton Anthology of Literature by Women* like a talisman, like a shield. Just so, they carry *The Woman Warrior;* they call it "the book." "We're studying the book in class." "Will you discuss the book with us?" I don't like all this overpraising of my daughter and rudeness toward my sons—especially since my writing has gotten better—wiser and more skillful—as I've gone along.

China Men was almost part of *The Woman Warrior;* I wrote much of those two books at the same time. I once meant for them to be one large book. But the women's stories and the men's stories parted into two volumes, naturally replicating history and geography: the women stayed in China and maintained communities; the men sailed off to the Gold Mountain, where they built Chinatowns. The Quality Paperback Club printed *The Woman Warrior* and *China Men* as a boxed set, the most correct presentation.

The use of myths in the two books is quite different. The myths and the lives in *The Woman Warrior* are integrated in the women's and girls' stories so that we cannot find the seams where the myth leaves off and a life and imagination begin. Fa Mu Lan is a fantasy that inspires the girls' psyches and their politics. The myths transform lives and are themselves changed.

In *China Men* the myths are separate from the men's adventures in the modern world. That book is like a six-layer club sandwich or cake. I tell six present-day stories, and between them are the myths. The men have trouble keeping Chinese ways in the new land. What good are the old stories? How can we live up to the ancestral heroes? What are myths anyway? Religious directives? Warnings? Amusing stories? Old-country baggage? Quest maps to the Gold Mountain? Why not be rid of the mythical, and be a free American?

Sinologists have criticized me for not knowing myths and for distorting them; pirates correct my myths, revising them to make them conform to some traditional Chinese version. They don't understand that myths have to change, be useful or be forgotten. Like the people who carry them across oceans, the myths become American. The myths I write are new, American. That's why they often appear as cartoons and kung fu movies. I take the power I need from whatever myth. Thus Fa Mu Lan has the words cut into her back; in traditional story, it is the man, Ngak Fei the Patriot, whose parents cut vows on his back. I mean to take his power for women.

I visited China after I'd written the mythic China that we in the West have made up. The actual China is much the way I imagined it and affirms the accuracy of talk-story. (It also brings up the philosophical problem of how to see through preconceptions.) If I could rewrite *The Woman Warrior,* though, I'd make some changes in setting: the well in "No Name Woman" is actually next to the Hong family temple. I'd write a scene of the men standing on its steps and teasing the girls; my mother was so flustered that she broke her jug. The other adjustment I'd make would be to bring living spaces closer together, house added upon house. Having always lived in the United States, I could not imagine how close the people in China crowd together. The "lanes" are alleys; you step over the raised threshold of the "great front door" on to dirt floors. The dwellings I've seen that most resemble my family's adobe villages are the pueblos in New Mexico and Arizona. A branch of our tribe lives in each room; everyone's behavior reverberates community-wide.

There are omissions that I'm sorry I didn't think of until long after I'd finished *The Woman Warrior*. I don't know why I didn't write down such obvious, important details. One is that Fa Mu Lan was a weaver. The chant begins with the sound of her shuttle and loom: "Jik jik jik" "Weave weave weave." I love it that *texture* and *text* come from the same root word. The other thing I wish I could add is that when Ts'ai Yen, the woman warrior who composed eighteen songs for the barbarian reed pipe, looked up in the sky, she saw home-flying geese that made formations of words—her letters home.[8]

KINGSTON ON HER CRITICS

When reading most of the reviews and critical analyses of *The Woman Warrior*, I have two reactions: I want to pat those critics on their backs, and I also giggle helplessly, shaking my head. (Helpless giggles turn less frequently into sobs as one gets older.) The critics did give my book the National Book Critics Circle Award; and they reviewed it in most of the major magazines and newspapers, thus publicizing it enough to sell. Furthermore, they rarely gave it an unfavorable review. I pat them on the back for recognizing good writing—but, unfortunately, I suspect most of them of perceiving its quality in an unconscious sort of way; they praise the wrong things.

Now, of course, I expected *The Woman Warrior* to be read from the women's lib angle and the Third World angle, the *Roots* angle; but it is up to the writer to transcend trendy categories. What I did not foresee was the critics measuring the book and me against the stereotype of the exotic, inscrutable, mysterious oriental. About two-thirds of the reviews did this. In some cases, I must admit, it was only a line or a marring word that made my stomach turn, the rest of the review being fairly sensible. You might say that I am being too thin-skinned; but a year ago I had really believed that the days of gross stereotyping were over, that the 1960s, the Civil Rights movement, and the end of the war in Vietnam enlightened America, if not in deeds at least in manners. Pridefully enough, I believed that I had written with such power that the reality and humanity of my characters would bust through any stereotypes of them. Simplemindedly, I wore a sweat-shirt for the dust-jacket photo, to deny the exotic. I had not calculated how blinding stereotyping is, how stupefying. The critics who said how the book was good because it was, or was not, like the oriental fantasy in their heads might as well have said how weak it was, since it in fact did not break through that fantasy.[9]

When Frank Chin was writing all this horrible stuff, he was also sending me voluminous letters which were really terrible. He talked about beating me up. They were threat letters. And so I answered a couple of his letters directly because I didn't want to do it publicly but I answered him directly. All I got back was more horrible stuff. Then I thought I do not want to waste any more of my energy in confrontations with Frank Chin. I was thinking, he was writing on a low karma level and if I write back to him, I'm not getting a worthy enough opponent in order to write great literature. I'm not going to honor him by making him my selected enemy and I'm not going to get good writing out of it. . . .

I would feel bad about [both the reviewers and the critics] but I never took them seriously. I think I never believed them. I always saw it as a smallness in those critics, a small mindedness that they would use me politically. It never occurred to me that they were right. . . . I felt that I had broken stereotypes and that I was writing really human characters. And I felt that the people who said I was writing stereotypes were really a lost cause because they themselves were not able to see through stereotypes.[10]

I don't think of it as a misunderstanding or a rift or anything that's between him [Chin] and me. It's always been him with these attacks, and I usually don't answer at all. He calls me terrible names such as race traitor. He even wrote me a letter that he's going to beat me up if he sees me. I don't want to honor him with answers. . . .

Actually, I've stopped reading his work, because I think he does not mean me well. I read for inspiration and life and help, and I don't think he wants to help me. What are the real important issues at stake? I have identified two. One of them is the racial and cultural myths. Whom do they belong to? Frank would say they belong to real Chinese such as himself. And they do not belong to, for example, the Caucasians. My feeling is, if somebody goes to a book store and buys my book, then they have bought the myths, and they can have the great myths of China by reading them. The only way that myths stay alive is if we pass them on. He has also been saying that there is a true text, including the chant of the Woman Warrior. Now I know that myth is not passed on by text; it's mostly passed on by word of mouth, and every time you tell a story and every time you hear it, it's different. So there isn't one frozen authentic version; there are many, many authentic versions different from person to person. . . .

[A]s a woman, it's absolutely clear to me that we have the freedom of creating alternate myths, and for Frank Chin, as a male, there is a monolith, one monument of a myth. The other difference—I just discovered this recently and am very surprised at this coincidence—I think he just published his translation of *The Art of War* [Sun Tzu, ca. 500 B. C., ascribed to Sun Wu], one of the traditional Chinese books of war. He's brought this into the world at the same time that I am writing my book of peace. You can see the fundamental difference in values.[11]

KINGSTON ON RACIAL STEREOTYPES

To say we are inscrutable, mysterious, exotic denies us our common humanness, because it says that we are so different from a regular human being that we are by our nature intrinsically unknowable. Thus the stereotyper aggressively defends ignorance. *Nor* do we want to be called *not* inscrutable, exotic, mysterious. These are false way of looking at us. We do not want to be measured by a false standard at all.

To call a people exotic freezes us into the position of always being alien—politically a most sensitive point with us because of the long history in America of the Chinese Exclusion Acts, the deportations, the law denying us citizenship when we have been part of America since its beginning. By giving the "oriental" (always Eastern, never *here*) inhuman, unexplainable qualities, the racist abrogates human qualities, and, carrying all this to extremes, finds it easier to lynch the Chinaman, bomb Japan, napalm Vietnam. "How amazing," they may as well be saying, "that she writes like a human being. How un-oriental." "I cannot understand her. It has to be her innate mystery." Blacks and women are making much better progress. I did not read any reviews of *Roots* that judged whether or not Alex Haley's characters ate watermelon or had rhythm. And there were only two cases I encountered of sexist stereotyping:

one from my home-town paper, *The Stockton Record:* "Mrs. Kingston is a 36-year-old housewife and mother who teaches creative writing and English." The above was a news story on *The Woman Warrior* winning the National Book Critics Circle Award, so the paper might have described me as a writer. The other was *Bookshelf,* a journal of Asian Studies: "The highly acclaimed first book by a Chinese-American school-teacher."

How stubbornly Americans hang on to the oriental fantasy can be seen in their picking "The White Tigers" chapter as their favorite. Readers tell me it ought to have been the climax. But I put it at the beginning to show that the childish myth is past, not the climax we reach for. Also, "The White Tigers" is not a Chinese myth but one transformed by America, a sort of kung fu movie parody.[12]

KINGSTON ON GLOBALISM

I was going to write against the minimalist novel in order to write a global novel. The reason I was thinking of a global novel was that I began to notice that every city that I went to anywhere in the world is a cosmopolitan city. You come to Beijing, London, anywhere, and you are surrounded by people from all over the world. Every country has had its diaspora and everybody is going everywhere, and so in order to write a story about any city, any American city or any other city, you have to be able to write characters from every cultural background. A story of a city is also the story of all the people on the entire planet. . . . There are really few tribes where there are people of just one race and one cultural background. Everybody is all mixed in together. Characters come from different linguistic backgrounds. I hear pieces of many languages. . . . If I write this novel in English the characters will have accents from all over the world. The novelist has to have an ear for the varieties of even one language. . . .

There are many constant diasporas from home countries, and when we are here, diasporas throughout the American continents. You know, the average American moves every four and a half years. And yet, the people of color have stronger senses of community than I imagine the average White person has. These can be communities that band together in hardship, the worst ones being gangs. But then there are also religious communities in the churches. There are China Towns, Asia Towns, family associations that were started 200 years ago when people first came here and they still flourish today. So, in one sense there is this falling apart, losing old languages, losing the old ways, but maybe not so much losing of the old values. . . .[13]

KINGSTON ON CHINESE AMERICANS

That we be called by our correct name is as important to any Chinese American as it is to native Americans, Blacks and any American minority that needs to define itself on its own terms. We should have been smart like the Americans of Japanese Ancestry, whose name explicitly spells out their American citizenship. (Semantics, however, did not save the AJAs from the camps.) Chinese-American history has been a battle for recognition as Americans; we have fought hard for the right to legal American citizenship. Chinese are those people who look like us in Hong Kong, the People's Republic and Taiwan. Apparently many Caucasians in America do not know that a person born in the USA is automatically American, no matter how he or she may look. Now we do call ourselves Chinese, and we call ourselves Chinamen, but when we say "I'm Chinese," it is in the context of differentiating ourselves from Japanese, for example. When we say we are Chinese, it is short for Chinese-Americans or ethnic Chinese; the "American" is implicit. I had hoped that this was the usage of the reviews, but instead there is a carelessness, an unawareness.

As for "Chinaman," I think we had better keep that word for use amongst ourselves, though people here in Hawaii do use it with no denigrating overtones as in the popular name for Mokolii, "Chinaman's Hat." And lately, I have been thinking that we ought to leave out the hyphen in "Chinese-American," because the hyphen gives the word on either side equal weight, as if linking two nouns. It looks as if a Chinese-American has double citizenship, which is impossible in today's world. Without the hyphen, "Chinese" is an adjective and "American" a noun; a Chinese American is a type of American. (This idea about the hyphen is my own, and I have not talked to anyone else who has thought of it; therefore, it is a fine point, "typical" of no one but myself.)

I hope that the above explanation makes clear why I and other Chinese Americans felt a clunk of imperfection when reading Peter S. Beagle's and Jane Kramer's otherwise fine pieces in *Harper's Bookletter* and *The New York Times Book Review* respectively. Both gathered from the dust-jacket, and perhaps from my name, that I had "married an American." Chinese Americans read that and I groaned "Oh, no!" immediately offended. I guess Caucasian Americans need to be told why. After all, I *am* married to an American. But to say so in summing up my life implies these kinds of things: that I married someone different from myself, that I somehow became *more* American through marriage, and that marriage is the way to assimilation. The phrase is too general. We suspect that they might mean, "She married a Caucasian." Too many people use those words interchangeably, "American" and "Caucasian." In some ways, it is all right to say that I am "Chinese" or my husband is "American" if they did not stop there but go on to show what has been left out. . . .

Sometimes you just have to laugh because there really is no malice, and they are trying their best. *Viva* magazine published the "No Name Woman" chapter with a full-page colour illustration of Japanese maidens at the window; they wear kimonos, lacquered hair-dos, and through the window is lovely, snow-capped Mt Fuji. Surprise, Asian brothers and sisters! We may as well think of ourselves as Asian Americans because we are all alike anyway. I did not feel angry until I pointed out the Japanese picture to some Caucasians who said, "It doesn't matter." (And yet, if an Asian American movement that includes Chinese, Japanese, Filipinos is possible, then solidarity with Caucasian Americans is possible.) I for one was raised with vivid stories about Japanese killing ten million Chinese, including my relatives, and was terrified of Japanese, especially AJAs, the only ones I had met.

It appears that when the critics looked at my book, they heard a jingle in their heads, "East is east and west is west. . . ." Yes, there were lazy literary critics who actually used that stupid Kipling British-colonial cliché to get a handle on my writing . . . I do not want the critics to decide whether or not the twain shall meet. I want them to be sensitive enough to know that they are not to judge Chinese American writing through the viewpoint of nineteenth-century British-colonial writing.[14]

KINGSTON ON THE CHINESE AMERICAN WRITER

I have never before read a critic who took a look at a Jewish American spouse and said, "There's something wrong with that Saul Bellow and Norman Mailer. They aren't at all like the one I'm married to." Critics do not ask whether Vonnegut is typical of German Americans; they do not ask whether J.P. Donleavy is typical of Irish Americans. You would never know by reading the reviews of Francine du Plessix

Gray's *Lovers and Tyrants* that it is by and about an immigrant from France. Books written by Americans of European ancestry are reviewed as American novels.

Now I agree with these critics—the book *is* "personal" and "subjective" and "singular." It may even be one-of-a-kind, unique, exceptional. I am not a sociologist who measures truth by the percentage of times behavior takes place. Those critics who do not explore why and how this book is different but merely point out its difference as a flaw have a very disturbing idea about the role of the writer. Why must I "represent" anyone besides myself? Why should I be denied an individual artistic vision? And I do not think I wrote a "negative" book, as the Chinese American reviewer said; but suppose I had? Suppose I had been so wonderfully talented that I wrote a tragedy? Are we Chinese Americans to deny ourselves tragedy? If we give up tragedy in order to make a good impression on Caucasians, we have lost a battle. Oh, well, I'm certain that some day when a great body of Chinese American writing becomes published and known, then readers will no longer have to put such a burden on each book that comes out. Readers can see the variety of ways for Chinese Americans to be.

(For the record, most of my mail is from Chinese American women, who tell me how similar their childhoods were to the one in the book, or they say their lives were not like that at all, but they understand the feelings; then they tell me some stories about themselves. Also, I was invited to Canada to speak on the role of the Chinese Canadian woman, and there was a half-page ad for the lecture in the Chinese language newspaper.)

The artistically interesting problem which the reviewers are really posing is: How much exposition is needed? There are so many levels of knowledge and ignorance in the audience. "It's especially hard for a non-Chinese," says Malloy, "and that's a troubling aspect of this book." A Chinese Canadian man writes in a letter, "How dare you make us sound like savages with that disgusting monkey feast story!" (Since publishing the book, I have heard from many monkey feast witnesses and participants.) Diane Johnson in *The New York Review of Books* says that there are fourth and fifth generation Chinese Americans who can't speak English. (It is more often the case that they can't speak Chinese. A fourth or fifth generation Chinese American and Caucasian American are not too different except in looks and history.) There is a reviewer who says it is amazing what I could do with my IQ of zero. (How clumsy the joke would be if I explained how IQ tests aren't valid because they are culturally biased against a non-English-speaking child.) There are Chinese American readers who feel slighted because I did not include enough history. (In my own review of Laurence Yep's *Child of the Owl* in the *Washington Post,* I praised him for his bravery in letting images stand with no exposition.) My own sister says, "You wrote the book for us—our family. It's how we are in everyday life. I have no idea what white people would make of it." Both my sisters say they laughed aloud.[15]

KINGSTON ON WRITING

All my characters are story-tellers, and I suspect that some of them are telling me fiction. So when I write their lives down is it fiction or non-fiction?

The reason people are confused about whether my books are fiction or non-fiction is that *I* keep asking this question. I say, Is this real? Is this true? The readers pick up on my asking, and they ask that because I've planted the question.

But the truth is I answer that question. I'm always very honest with the reader. If I experience something for myself, I say I saw this. For example, I wanted to write about my grandfather, whom I never met. I think that's a problem typical of the biographer who writes about historical figures. I had to try to find a direct contact some-how. I didn't know him, so I approached him as a character by describing his brothers whom I knew. Well, I was only about two years old. I had no intellectual capacity for knowing them. And I wasn't even that interested in them. I *was* interested in their horses. So I described their horses. And I didn't even know the horses, so I described them as a metaphor of the night. This is from the point of view of a person who had direct contact, a toddler.

The other way of knowing my grandfather was my mother. I admit that to the reader: I say, I know because I have heard from her. Then it's my task to describe her personality, so when the reader reads about my grandfather, I expect him to under-stand we're looking through my mom looking at my grandfather. And each of these characters is delineated.

I suppose people get confused. But only because most biographers aren't con-stantly reminding us *how* they know.[16]

I am a solitary writer even among the community of writers. I am not sure what the direct effect of others' writing has on my writing. So far, when writing in commu-nity the work goes faster. I can feel our group energy pushing me to work better. Writing alone, I'm very slow. So that's one good effect. The veterans are writing the most wonderful, strong stories. We pull the stories out of one another with our intense listening. . . . I do believe that our lives and our art go together. Who I am and what I write are the same. *The Woman Warrior* is about a young girl trying to come to an understanding of herself; she is still individuating, she is learning what is secret and what is public. I wrote with the privacy of writing a diary. What I am writing now is about public life and about communal life, and so I set up the outside world to be the same as my inside world. . . . I feel that the writing process doesn't just begin when you are putting words on paper. It begins in the living that you do before, and I feel powerful enough now so that I can set up my daily living circumstances in order to support me and support my art. I do a lot of this by instinct, like bringing the vet-erans together. I don't figure it out until later. . . . The way I've looked at it is that I want to write about myself and other people in the truest way possible. To write a true autobiography or biography, I have to know what the other person dreams and how her imagination works. I am less interested in dates and facts. . . .

I don't do all my writing in the community. Much of my writing is in solitude, but I feel that it's vital that periodically there be this gathering of communal energy. It inspires me and I go back into solitude. It's like a wave—you know the wave goes out and comes to shore. This writing in community is a new discovery for me. I've spent too many years carrying writing as if it were a burden that's only mine. I want to tell everybody, and young people too, that there are many things that we must do in community. I wish I had started sooner.[17]

When I write most deeply, fly the highest, reach the furthest, I write like a dia-rist—that is, my audience is myself. I dare to write anything because I can burn my papers at any moment. I do not begin with the thought of an audience peering over my shoulder, nor do I find my being understood a common occurrence anyway—a miracle when it happens. My fantasy is that this self-indulgence will be good enough for the great American novel. Pragmatically, though, since my audience would have to be all America, I work on intelligibility and accessibility in a second draft. How-ever, I do not slow down to give boring exposition, which is information that is avail-able in encyclopedias, history books, sociology, anthropology, mythology. (After all, I am not writing history or sociology but a "memoir" like Proust, as Christine Cook in the *Hawaii Observer* and Diane Johnson in *The New York Review of Books* are clever enough to see. I am, as Diane Johnson says, "slyly writing a memoir, a form which . . . can neither [be] dismiss[ed] as fiction nor quarrel[ed] with as fact." "But the structure is a grouping of memoirs," says Christine Cook. "It is by definition a series of stories or anecdotes to illuminate the times rather than be autobiographical.") I rarely repeat anything that can be found in other book. Some readers will just have to do some background reading. Maybe my writing can provide work for English majors. Readers ought not to expect reading always to be as effortless as watching television.

I want my audience to include everyone. I had planned that if I could not find an American publisher, I would send the manuscript to Britain, Hong Kong, Canada, Taiwan—anywhere—and if it did not then find a publisher, I would keep it safe for posthumous publication. So I do believe in the timelessness and universality of individual vision. It would not just be a family book or an American book or a woman's book but a world book, and, at the same moment, my book.

The audience of *The Woman Warrior* is also very specific. For example, I address Chinese Americans twice, once at the beginning of the book and once at the end. I ask some questions about what life is like for you, and, happily, you answer. Chinese Americans have written that I explain customs they had not understood. I even write for my old English professors of the new criticism school in Berkeley, by incorporating what they taught about the structure of the novel. I refer to Virginia Woolf, Elizabeth Barrett Browning, Shakespeare; but those who are not English majors and don't play literary games will still find in those same sentences the other, main, important meanings. There are puns for Chinese speakers only, and I do not point them out for non-Chinese speakers. There are some visual puns best appreciated by those who write Chinese. I've written jokes in that book so private, only I can get them; I hope I sneaked them in unobtrusively so nobody feels left out. I hope my writing has many layers, as human beings have layers.[18]

I think that I contended with these questions [about language] when I was about 7 years old, and, you know, my first language is Chinese, and I only knew people who spoke Chinese. I talked story and I invented poems and made up songs and I heard stories, but when I began to know the English language and somewhere around 8 years old, I started to write, and the English language was so . . . [b]right, full of freedom. I felt freedom because the English language is so easy, and I thought, My gosh, everything I can hear I can notate it! I can notate Chinese. I can write Chinese in English. I can write English in English and I never had that power when I spoke only Chinese. You speak Chinese and then the written language is completely different. There's no system. It's one word at a time. But all of a sudden, with the 26 letters in the English alphabet you can write anything, so I just felt I had the most powerful tool, and I felt free to express myself.[19]

KINGSTON ON WRITING AND MEMORY

The artist's memory winnows out; it edits for what is important and significant. Memory, my own memory, shows me what is unforgettable, and helps me to get to an essence that will not die, and that haunts me until I can put it into a form, which is the writing. I don't want to get confused by making new memories on top of the old ones which were already such a large vision—the mythic China. Going to China would have meant the creation of, and the beginning of, another memory. . . . I have learned that writing does not make ghosts go away. I wanted to record, to find the words for, the "ghosts," which are only visions. They are not concrete; they are beautiful, and powerful. But they don't have a solidity that we can pass around from one to another. I wanted to give them a substance that goes beyond me. . . .

[M]emory is really nothing. It's not substantial, and it's not present. It has to do with past times, and in that sense, it's significant, except when it haunts you and when it is a foundation for the rest of the personality. Somehow, though, words are a medium to get to the seemingly subconscious.

I think that these visions don't just come full-blown and with details such as chairs and clothes, and where everything is placed—the relationships between bodies in a room. All that becomes more and more accessible as I approach them with words. Words clarify the vision and memory.

When you think about it, words are also insignificant, insubstantial, not things. So we can use them to arrive at insignificant, insubstantial memories. As I paint part of a vision, the next part of it becomes clear. It's as if I am building the underpinnings of a bridge, and then I can cross it, and see more and more clearly. . . .

Because then you find the next memory, all of the time keeping an eye on what's happening in real life, right now. I think that my stories have a constant breaking in and out of the present and past. So the reader might be walking along very well in the present, and vice-versa. The reason that we remember a past moment at all is that our present-day life is still a working-out of a similar situation. . . . Understanding the past changes the present. And the ever-evolving present changes the significance of the past.[20]

I don't want to regurgitate. Writing should be constantly an act of creation and going forward into the new. But I've been thinking a lot about loss and memory because my father died just before the fire, so there was that loss of my father and then the loss of the house and the loss of the book. Everything happened at once. But everybody has losses. Working with veterans, I understand now that mourning is never over. We will always have mourning after a traumatic event; after a loss there will always be mourning. We want it that way because we don't want to forget our feelings for that person or that thing. However, the mourning changes; mourning breaks up into different elements. We will mourn in different ways and one way of mourning, perhaps you pass a spot or you go under a tree and you remember a person that you talked to under that tree. That's his spirit visiting you. That remembrance and that happiness are mourning, too, transformed.[21]

KINGSTON ON READING

I think that if a person doesn't read, maybe they cannot come out of themselves. . . . I think [there is] a growth process of human development . . . first there is an awareness of the ego, the self, and then of another and many others to become a communal person. And we need to go even beyond that—our family, tribe, Chinatown, gang, nation—into a larger selflessness or agape. I think it is a very rare person who will take on public and global responsibilities. They don't even go out to vote, and you only have to do that once in two years. Reading and writing should expand and transform the self. . . . I just read about scientists who measured the strands of neuropeptides in our brains. They found that in the people who are most educated and who consistently read books, the strands actually get longer. In the brains of the ones who don't read, the neuropeptides get shorter. We physically change because of our reading and thinking, and then I hope we become strong enough to create a good society around us. Reading must be an essential tool for envisioning and making the world.[22]

NOTES

1. Donna Perry, "Maxine Hong Kingston," in *Backtalk: Women Writers Speak Out, Interviews by Donna Perry* (New Brunswick, N.J.: Rutgers University Press, 1993), p. 180.

2. Diane Simmons, "A Conversation with Maxine Hong Kingston," in *Maxine Hong Kingston* (New York: Twayne, 1999), pp. 166–167.

3. Neila C. Seshachari, "Reinventing Peace: Conversations with Tripmaster Maxine Hong Kingston," in *Conversations with Maxine Hong Kingston,* edited by Paul Skenazy and Tera Martin (Jackson: University Press of Mississippi, 1998), pp. 192–193.

4. Maxine Hong Kingston, quoted in Simmons, *Maxine Hong Kingston,* p. 3.

5. Seshachari, "Reinventing Peace: Conversations with Tripmaster Maxine Hong Kingston," pp. 193–194, 195–196.

6. Simmons, "A Conversation with Maxine Hong Kingston," p. 165.

7. Kingston, "Useful Education," in *Hawai'i One Summer* (Honolulu: University of Hawaii Press, 1998), pp. 41–45.

8. Kingston, "Personal Statement," in *Approaches to Teaching Kingston's The Woman Warrior,* edited by Shirley Geok-lin Lim (New York: Modern Language Association, 1991), pp. 23–25.

9. Kingston, "Cultural Mis-readings by American Reviewers," in *Asian and Western Writers in Dialogue,* edited by Guy Amirthanayagam (London: Macmillan, 1982), p. 55.

10. Kingston, quoted in Simmons, *Maxine Hong Kingston,* pp. 40–41.

11. Seshachari, "Reinventing Peace: Conversations with Tripmaster Maxine Hong Kingston," pp. 202–203.

12. Kingston, "Cultural Mis-readings by American Reviewers," p. 57.

13. Seshacari, "Reinventing Peace: Conversations with Tripmaster Maxine Hong Kingston," pp. 194–195, 209.

14. Kingston, "Cultural Mis-readings by American Reviewers," pp. 59–60, 61.

15. Ibid., pp. 55–65.

16. Phyllis Hoge Thompson, "This is the Story I Heard: A Conversation with Maxine Hong Kingston and Earll Kingston," *Biography,* 6, no. 1 (1983): 4.

17. Seshachari, "Reinventing Peace: Conversations with Tripmaster Maxine Hong Kingston," pp. 197–198, 199.

18. Kingston, "Cultural Mis-readings by American Reviewers," pp. 64–65.

19. Seshachari, "Reinventing Peace: Conversations with Tripmaster Maxine Hong Kingston," p. 207.

20. Paula Rabinowitz, "Eccentric Memories: A Conversation With Maxine Hong Kingston," in *Conversations with Maxine Hong Kingston,* pp. 67–69.

21. Seshachari, "Reinventing Peace: Conversations with Tripmaster Maxine Hong Kingston," pp. 200–201.

22. Ibid., p. 213.

AUTOBIOGRAPHICAL WRITING

When they were first published, both *The Woman Warrior* and *China Men* attracted a great deal of attention from critics who study autobiography. Kingston's work has altered the nature of this genre, which had before been defined by classic works of American literature such as Benjamin Franklin's autobiography, the first complete edition of which was published in 1868. Classic autobiography tells the life story of some notable individual, someone whose life has been particularly significant in political or historical terms. The story develops chronologically, from earliest memories and childhood experiences through the mature achievements, in some cases ending with an account of the circumstances that led the subject to write his or her life story. Kingston's autobiographical work is obviously quite different from this classical model. Her subject does not possess obvious historical or political significance—she writes about her experiences as a young Chinese American girl attempting to reconcile the conflicting demands made upon her by her Chinese ancestry and everyday American life. To represent the pressures of this cross-cultural life, Kingston blends stories with myths and legends, blurring the boundary between the imaginative and the real. The narrative does not follow a clear chronological progression from childhood through to maturity; rather, it jumps forward and backward in time, from China to America, from the lives of her mother, father, and other relatives to her own present-day experiences.

The innovation Kingston brought to the form of the autobiography is matched by innovation in subject matter. The life she portrays derives significance not from some external measure such as historical importance or public popularity but from its intrinsic qualities. In this respect Kingston's work is similar to that of other minority authors who have written autobiographical narratives in order to assert the importance and significance of lives that are otherwise invisible to main-

Kingston

stream society. These include the writers of slave autobiographies, such as Frederick Douglass and Harriet Jacobs, as well as those who have followed in the tradition of slave narratives, such as the contemporary African American authors Toni Morrison and Maya Angelou. Hispanics such as the Chicana Sandra Cisneros, the Chicano Richard Rodriguez, and the Puerto Rican Judith Ortiz Cofer have also written autobiographies. It is not only the issue of race or ethnicity that sets Kingston's work apart from classical autobiography but also that of gender. The case has been made that women's autobiography is quite different from that of men. Whereas men have historically occupied positions of power and influence that have had obvious significance for the progress of history, women until recently have been denied this participation in the public world. Consequently, women have had difficulty perceiving their lives as significant when they have lived predominantly in the domestic realm. The value of a woman's life and the reasons why that life should be told as a literary narrative are not matters that can be simply assumed by any woman writer.

In her study *A Poetics of Women's Autobiography: Marginality and the Fictions of Self-Representation* (1987) the critic Sidonie Smith places Kingston's work within a tradition of feminine autobiography that goes back to the fifteenth-century English mystic Margery Kempe and develops through the writing of Margaret Cavendish, Duchess of Newcastle, in the seventeenth century, to the work of Charlotte Charke in the eighteenth century and that of the nineteenth-century philosopher Harriet Martineau. Smith argues that these writers have all contested the prevailing ideas of what a woman is and what her life should be by presenting themselves and their lives as a challenge to dominant definitions of femininity. She singles out *The Woman Warrior* from other contemporary autobiographies because, in her view, it "exemplifies the potential for works from the marginalized to challenge the ideology of individualism and with it the ideology of gender." Smith continues: "Recognizing the inextricable relationship between an individual's sense of 'self' and the community's stories of selfhood, Kingston self-consciously reads herself into existence through the stories her culture tells about women. Using autobiography to create identity, she breaks down the hegemony of formal 'autobiography' and breaks out of the silence that has bound her culturally to discover a resonant voice of her own."[1] Kingston engages not only the mainstream American ideas of what a woman should be but also the ideas of womanhood that are part of the Chinese minority culture of her parents.

Boy at a streetside butcher's stall in San Francisco's Chinatown, circa 1895–1906. Photograph by Arnold Genthe.

Kingston's interest in writing in an autobiographical style, according to Smith, is to engage repressive definitions of femininity and, by first exposing and then rejecting these dominant definitions, actively to seek a definition of self that is authentic. What Smith does not question is the notion of historical truth that is an important component of classic autobiography. Autobiographical writing is assumed by readers to be historically truthful rather than the invented work of the writer's imagination. Kingston has remarked that all the material that went into the writing of *The Woman Warrior* and *China Men* was either a part of her culture or a part of her family's experience; in either case, she did not invent any of the characters, circumstances, or events represented in the books. This claim to objective truthfulness and accuracy has led some Asian American critics to denounce Kingston's autobiographical work as unrepresentative of Chinese experience, inaccurate in its use of traditional Chinese myths, and reliant upon western stereotypes of exotic Orientals. In her 1992 essay "Autobiography as Guided Chinatown Tour? Maxine Hong Kingston's *The Woman Warrior* and the Chinese American Autobiographical Controversy," Sau-ling Cynthia Wong explains that the reason why Kingston's book has become controversial is that Asian critics envision Caucasian readers interpreting the narrative as a true account of

China and of Chinese American culture. While other Chinese Americans can see that the book is a special kind of autobiography, based upon inherited stories and impressions and recollections, Western readers lack the insight into the reality of Chinese American culture necessary to see where invention stops and historical reality begins. According to some of Kingston's critics, such as Frank Chin, this limited insight is owing to the form of the autobiography, which is essentially Western and Christian rather than Chinese. Wong sums up the failings of which Kingston has been accused by Chin and others: "the autobiographer's work should be innocent of material that might be seized upon by unsympathetic outsiders to illustrate prevalent stereotypes of the ethnic group; the author should stress the diversity of experience within the group and the uniqueness and self-definition of the individual. Ideally, an ethnic autobiography should also be a history in microcosm of the community, especially of its sufferings, struggles, and triumphs over racism." Kingston's failing, according to this view, is her emphasis upon her own unique experience and that of her individual family members at the expense of the communal experience of Chinese Americans as a group. Wong paraphrases this argument: "an ethnic autobiographer should be an exemplar and spokesperson whose life will inspire the writer's own people as well as enlighten the ignorant about social truths."[2] She goes on, however, to point out that this requirement that ethnic autobiography be both representative and an invariably positive representation of ethnic experience conflicts with the desire of minority writers to claim the right to self-definition and self-representation through their writing. This desire is denied when the writer is obliged by her race to suppress negative experiences and to conform to a self-definition that is dictated by the ethnic community. Sociology comes to dominate over the expression of individual uniqueness. Wong observes the irony of a situation in which Kingston's autobiographical writing is attacked by Chinese American critics not because it is "insufficiently factual but [because] it is insufficiently fictional"—she has failed to alter and to edit her life to satisfy the demand for a positive portrayal of Chinese culture.[3]

TRUTH AND FICTION

"Be careful what you say. It comes true. It comes true. I had to leave home in order to see the world logically, logic the new way of seeing. I learned to think that mysteries are for explanation. I enjoy the simplicity. Concrete pours out of my mouth to cover the forests with freeways and sidewalks. Give me plastics, periodical tables, t.v. dinners with vegetables no more complex than peas mixed with diced carrots. Shine floodlights into dark corners: no ghosts."

Maxine Hong Kingston

From *The Woman Warrior: Memoirs of a Girlhood Among Ghosts* (New York: Knopf, 1976), p. 204.

In "Autobiography in a Different Voice: *The Woman Warrior* and the Question of Genre," Joan Lidoff argues that the style of autobiography written by Kingston and others, such as Mary Catherine Bateson and Kim Chernin, is characterized by precisely the attempt to represent the self in relation to others. Lidoff claims that contemporary "women's autobiographies are often written as biography." She explains that this "form of female autobiography validates a speaking voice by placing it in the service of another; it does not place itself center stage but understands itself in context by trying to recreate the parent as other—to see the mother in her own terms and not just as mother."[4] Seen in these terms, Kingston's autobiographical writing is an attempt to understand herself by understanding her parents: her mother in *The Woman Warrior* and her father in *China Men*. Rather than place herself at the center of the narrative, she adopts a self-effacing stance and places her family in the foreground. By presenting her life as part of the generations of women in her family and by presenting these women primarily through her mother's stories, Kingston blends the genres of fiction, mythology, lyric, history, and biography into a new form of autobiography in which the whole concept of truth or accuracy becomes ambiguous. Her fantasies are true, her mother's stories are true—even in the multiple versions that differ according to time, place, and audience—and memories are true, but in a private and subjective rather than an historical sense. This ambiguity reflects Kingston's resentment of her mother's confusion of fact and fiction; in *The Woman Warrior* the narrator shouts at her mother, "I don't want to listen to any more of your stories; they have no logic. They scramble me up. You lie with stories. . . . I can't tell what's real and what you make up" (202).

In the essay "Metaphors and Myths of Cross-Cultural Literacy: Autobiographical Narratives by Maxine Hong Kingston, Richard Rodriguez, and Malcolm X," Shirley K. Rose discusses Kingston's writing as racial autobiography. Writing one's life is a way of creating one's own reality within the context of society's construction of reality through cultural myths and metaphors. This process has particular significance for the minority writer who seeks to understand the social prejudices and forms of discrimination that constitute external reality and that impinge upon the personal construction of subjective reality. Rose focuses on the theme of the acquisition of literacy in racial autobiography and highlights two aspects of this theme: first, the role of literacy in the achievement of individual autonomy, and second, literacy as a means for social participation. She explains the relationship between these two functions of literacy: "The writer who claims autonomy reinforces his participation in a culture when he exploits its conventions for literate discourse. The writer who describes her participation in literate culture constructs an autonomous self in the act of writing."[5] These complementary functions of literacy Rose finds in Kingston's work as well as in the autobiographical writing of Malcolm X (*The Autobiography of Malcolm X*, 1965) and Richard Rodriguez (*Hunger of Memory*, 1981). The cross-cultural positioning of these writers located them at the margins of literate American culture, but the power to write their own lives gave them access to personal autonomy and also permitted participation in mainstream culture. As Rose concludes, these writers "create cultural roles for themselves. They read and write their own lives."[6]

ASIAN AMERICAN LITERATURE

Kingston's books are firmly located within the growing body of works by Chinese American women writers such as Jade Snow Wong, Amy Tan, and Gish Jen. Kingston has named Wong as an early and formative influence upon her writing because Wong's autobiographical novel *Fifth Chinese Daughter*, published in 1945, showed her that literary works could be written and published that featured a Chinese American girl as the protagonist. Before encountering Wong's book, Kingston's assumptions about what was possible in literature had been shaped by the Caucasian heroes and heroines about whom she read. Tan, in novels such as *The Joy Luck Club* (1989) and *The Kitchen God's Wife* (1991), and Jen, in *Typical American* (1991) and *Mona in the Promised Land* (1996), write of the conflicts and tensions that characterize relations between American-born daughters and their Chinese immigrant mothers. Though neither Tan nor Jen explicitly employs the autobiographical form that Kingston has used, both draw extensively upon their own cross-cultural experiences in depicting the quest for personal identity amid conflicting cultural demands and family pressures.

Amy Ling describes some of the Chinese American writers who preceded Kingston in her essays "Chinese American Women Writers: The Tradition behind Maxine Hong Kingston" and "Chinamerican Women Writers: Four Forerunners of Maxine Hong Kingston." The writers Ling discusses are the sisters Edith and Winnifred Eaton, Mai-mai Sze, and Huang Chua. The Eaton sisters chose to write under pseudonyms: Edith published as Sui Sin Far and Winnifred as Onoto Watanna. Whereas Far claimed her Chinese ancestry in stories and articles that exposed the discrimination confronted by Chinese Americans, Watanna claimed a false Japanese lineage and wrote romantic stories set in exotic Japanese set-

Dust jacket for Amy Tan's 1991 novel, a fictionalized biography of her mother

tings. In the stories collected in *Mrs. Spring Fragrance* (1912) Far attempted to break the destructive stereotypes of Chinese men and women by representing them as complex and sympathetic individuals, while pointing ironically to the prejudice with which these people are received in mainstream society. Rather than openly contest the racist stereotypes of Orientals, Watanna engaged these popular stereotypes to present variations of romantic formula fiction in which a frail and delicate Oriental woman is won by a strong and powerful European man. Still, in books such as *A Japanese Nightingale* (1901) and *The Love of Azalea* (1904) Watanna represented a contrast between the physical frailty of her heroines and their emotional and psychological strength.

In the work of the Eaton sisters, according to Ling, there is an awareness of the inferior status of women within both mainstream Western society and the subculture of the Chinese American community. This awareness produced what Ling calls, following the African American writer W. E. B. Du Bois, "double consciousness." This term names the experience of perceiving oneself to be a unique and distinctive individual but having this individuality denied by others who perceive members of ethnic minorities through the lens of racial stereotype. Both Sze and Chua write out of this experience of "double consciousness." In her autobiography, *Echo of a Cry* (1945), Sze tells of her early childhood spent in China and then reports in detail what Ling terms "the process of anglicization" she underwent first in England and later in the United States.[7] While she failed to fit into the Western society in which she found herself, Sze also discovered that upon her return to China, she was out of place there, too, because of her Western attitudes and values. She became deracinated—a foreigner both in China and America. The same experience of losing one's nationality and with it the sense of belonging in the world is the central theme of Chua's *Crossings* (1968). The "crossings" of the title refer to the ocean crossings made by the heroine as she travels between America and France, but the title also refers to the cultural crossings, the movement between languages, and even the emotional crossings the heroine, Jane, is required to make between her parents: her father, who is able to accept his Caucasian daughter-in-law, and her mother, who cannot. Jane finds her sense of self undermined by her inability to identify satisfactorily with either China or the West; she says that she has loved China and America "separately but equally,"[8] yet she belongs to neither, and her "double consciousness" is a consequence of her dual heritage. In this respect, *Crossings* is an important precursor to Kingston's explorations of the experience of cross-cultural identity.

In the more expansive context of her book-length study of Chinese American women writers, *Between Worlds: Women Writers of Chinese Ancestry* (1990), Ling is able to compare Kingston's work at length with such writers as Jade Snow Wong and Tan. Ling acknowledges that the autobiographies by Wong and Kingston are quite different, but she points out that, nonetheless, the condition of cross-cultural consciousness or double consciousness affects both writers and is represented in their writing. Whereas *Fifth Chinese Daughter* was written primarily for a white audience during World War II and presented the power of opportunity available even to an oppressed Chinese woman in America, *The Woman Warrior* was written in the aftermath of the Civil Rights movement and the women's liberation movement of the 1960s and 1970s. As Patricia Lin Blinde points out in her essay on Kingston and Wong, "The Icicle in the Desert: Perspective and Form in the Works of Two Chinese-American Women Writers," Wong's work tends to follow the rags-to-riches pattern of the paradigmatic American dream, made popular in late-nineteenth-century fiction by Horatio Alger's novels. Blinde argues, "The popular view that the Chinese are a hard-working, education-oriented and thrifty people is itself a framework that lends itself well to the Horatio Alger paradigm. Coupled with the belief that with hard work and sacrifice anyone (not least of all a Chinese woman) can achieve success in America, the

KINGSTON AT AN ASIAN AMERICAN WRITERS' CONFERENCE

"Voice after voice telling all manner of things, by Saturday, I found myself saying my own work inside my head to counteract certain poets. My ears and head and body rejected their beats, which I also tried to cancel by tapping out my own rhythms with a finger. I felt like Johnny-Got-His-Gun, paralyzed except for that one finger. Earll, my husband, was reciting Yeats's poetry to himself, as an antidote."

Maxine Hong Kingston

From "Talk Story: A Writers' Conference," in *Hawai'i One Summer* (Honolulu: University of Hawaii Press, 1998), p. 50.

individual about whom the autobiography is being written is him/herself reduced to a type, i.e. endowed with character traits which ensure success."[9] Kingston's, then, "is a much more personal text, written not as an exemplum for others but as a means of exorcising the personal ghosts that haunt the author."[10] If the two books are different in tone and attitude—the one restrained and polite, the other angry and rebellious—they are also quite different in form, as Ling explains: "*Fifth Chinese Daughter* is a sober, straightforward narrative delivered in chronological order, as though to tell this much were effort enough. *The Woman Warrior* is poetic, experimental, fragmented in narrative line, a virtuoso performance of imaginative power and verbal dexterity."[11] But both Wong and Kingston are American-born daughters of immigrant parents from southern China who sought to bridge their dual inheritance and to reconcile the conflicting demands made upon them by China and America, by East and West. Both had impressed upon them by their parents the sense that they were living only temporarily in America and would one day return to China; both found their parents' traditional beliefs and values embarrassing; both attempted to reconcile conflicting self-images; and both struggled with silence and the difficulty of articulating their ideas in order to realize an authentic sense of self.

Whereas Kingston claims Wong as in some respects her literary mentor and inspiration, Ling sees a close relationship between Kingston's work and Tan's fiction, especially *The Joy Luck Club,* which Ling describes as being "in parts an echo and a response and in parts a continuation and expansion" of *The Woman Warrior.*[12] In her representation of two generations of Chinese American women—American-born daughters and their immigrant mothers—Tan continues Kingston's exploration of the tensions that characterize the mother-daughter relation: "The daughters are proud of their mothers' strength and ingenuity; moved by their tragic, beautiful stories from the Old Country, and touched by their fierce love; but at the same time the daughters are exasperated by their mothers' impossible demands; resentful of their mothers' intrusions on their lives, and sometimes humiliated and ashamed of their stubborn, superstitious, out-of-place Old World ways."[13] The alienation of children from their parents and the difficulty of bridging this separation connects Tan's writing with that of Kingston. Indeed, the need for reconciliation is what links the work of Wong and Tan with that of Kingston, as Ling observes: "one cannot cling solely to the new American ways and reject the old Chinese ways, for that is the way of the child. One must reconcile the two and make one's peace with the old."[14]

Shirley Geok-lin Lim uses the wider context of Asian American literature to explore the issue of self-definition in a multicultural context in her essay "Twelve Asian American Writers: In Search of Self-Definition." In this essay Kingston is cited as one of many Asian American writers who seek through literature to negotiate the tensions between two cultures. Lim compares Kingston's treatment of male-dominated or patriarchal attitudes with that of Wong in *Fifth Chinese Daughter* and of Jeanne Wakatsuki Houston and James D. Houston in *Farewell to Manzanar* (1973); she also compares Kingston's representation of the Asian immigrant experience and history with that of David Henry Hwang in his plays. Lim remarks that the predominance of history, biography, and autobiography in this body of writing is due to the interest in recording "personal experiences, social observations, and memory." She continues: "Works as varied as Pardee Lowe's, Monica Sone's and the Houstons' autobiographies, Toshio Mori's short stories, John Okada's and Louis Chu's novels, and Kingston's histories share a concern with sociological texture in their attempts to rewrite the past; as such, they exhibit in different degrees a burden of referentiality in which the texts demand to be read for their relevance to historical meaning."[15] Lim includes Kingston with Chin and Jeffrey Paul Chan in the group of Asian American writers who are distinctly self-conscious and sensitive to their own literary voices, who "have begun to deal with problems of textuality instead of with racial stereotypes."[16]

RACE, GENDER, AND POSTMODERNISM

Kingston is most commonly discussed together with writers whose work focuses upon the twin issues of race and gender. For example, Jeanne R. Smith opens her essay "Rethinking American Culture: Maxine Hong Kingston's *Tripmaster Monkey*" with a comparison between Kingston and writers such as Alice Walker, Louise Erdrich, Toni Morrison, and Leslie Marmon Silko who draw on the rich storytelling traditions of African American and Native American cultures just as Kingston draws upon Chinese American oral traditions.[17] *The Woman Warrior* has

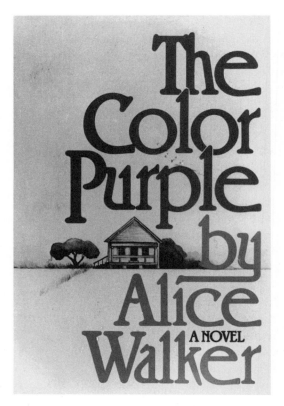

Dust jacket for Alice Walker's Pulitzer Prize-winning 1982 novel. Like Kingston's *The Woman Warrior*, the novel presents the lives of women silenced by a patriarchal culture.

been compared with Walker's *The Color Purple* (1982) in terms of a common concern with storytelling and its opposite: the silences imposed upon women in patriarchal culture. Both narratives explore the theme of an imposed feminine silence that has been broken. King-Kok Cheung, in the essay "'Don't Tell': Imposed Silences in *The Color Purple* and *The Woman Warrior*," observes that both narratives open with parental warnings. In Walker's novel Celie's stepfather warns of the dire consequences that would follow should she tell anyone about his sexual abuse of her; Kingston's mother warns her that she must keep secret the story of her aunt's illegitimate pregnancy and subsequent suicide. Both Celie and the narrator in *The Woman Warrior* confront racial, sexual, and linguistic obstacles that they nonetheless surmount; through speech and writing they not only survive but also eventually triumph. Cheung explains: "They work their way from speechlessness to eloquence not only by covering the historical stages women writers have traveled—from suffering patriarchy, to rebelling against its conventions, to creating their own ethos—but also by developing a style that emerges from their respective cultures. In the course of their odysseys, the destructive weapon of tradition is turned into a creative implement, and speech impediment becomes literary invention."[18] In overcoming the silences imposed upon women and telling their tales authentically, both writers use the dialect of their ethnic community rather than standard English and draw upon oral traditions in which women have always taken an important part; what they create is a distinctive style of expression that is both inherited and innovative. Walker rehabilitates the epistolary style as a means of feminist expression, and Kingston revises the autobiographical form to the same purpose. Thus, race and gender operate together to create the conditions for literary invention as well as for self-discovery. As Cheung argues, "Gender and ethnicity—inhibitive forces when these texts open—eventually become the sources of personal and stylistic strengths."[19]

Walker has suffered the same kind of attacks on her writing by African American men as Kingston faced from Chinese American male critics. Both have been charged with presenting distorted images of their ethnic cultures. Critics such as Ishmael Reed accused Walker of presenting African American men as brutal and violent, much as Chin claimed that Kingston played to the stereotypes of Chinese that underpin white racism. Both Walker and Kingston have been blamed for failing to repress in their writings the ugly or negative aspects of their experience as women within their specific racial groups; they have also been blamed for failing to be representative of African Americans or Chinese Americans. These male critics essentially demanded that Walker and Kingston place their racial allegiance above their feminist concerns about the oppressed position of women not only in mainstream American society but also within ethnic subcultures as well. Of course, Walker and Kingston have refused to choose between their ethnic and gender identities; they have refused to give priority to either racism or sexism, instead seeking to contest the structures of oppression that generate both racial and gender discrimination.

Kingston's most vociferous critic has been Chin; in the essay "The Production of Chinese American Tradition: Displacing American Orientalist Discourse," David Leiwei Li develops an extended comparison between *The Woman Warrior* and Chin's "Confessions of the Chinatown Cowboy." Li observes that the controversy between Chin and Kingston arose out of their desire to participate as Chinese Americans in the American literary canon. However, this desire has been frustrated and complicated by uncertainty about the form and theme that canonical texts should adopt. Li describes the nature of this uncertainty by using two contrasting concepts, which he terms "American Orientalist discourse" and "Chinese American discourse." The former describes and crystallizes the prejudiced attitude toward the Chinese as "heathen" and "barbarians" that produced anti-Asian immigration laws in the late nineteenth century; the latter term describes the language and conceptual vocabulary of Chinese immigrant culture in America. These two discourses coexist and have done so since the mid nineteenth century, with

MAGICAL REALISM

"When we Chinese girls listened to the adults talking-story, we learned that we failed if we grew up to be but wives or slaves. We could be heroines, swordswomen. Even if she had to rage across all China, a swordswoman got even with anybody who hurt her family. Perhaps women were once so dangerous that they had to have their feet bound."

Maxine Hong Kingston

From *The Woman Warrior: Memoirs of a Girlhood Among Ghosts* (New York: Knopf, 1976), p. 19.

American Orientalist discourse dominant as the expression of mainstream racism and Chinese American discourse existing as a form of resistance to these racist views and values. According to Li's argument, these discourses also provide the terms within which debate about the nature of Chinese American literary expression takes place. Thus, contemporary Chinese American writers must "confront the dual burden of at once subverting an American Orientalist discourse based on their cultural oppression and reconstructing a Chinese American tradition that would mark their cultural liberation."[20] In his discussion of the work of Kingston and Chin, Li shows how these writers do precisely this—displace an oppressive American Orientalist discourse and create a new Chinese American discourse within which to locate their own selves and their ethnic community.

Kingston has compared her writing with that of Morrison and Silko; with these writers she shares an interest in the interconnections that link racial and gender oppression, though they approach them from quite distinct perspectives: Morrison from an African American perspective, Silko from a Native American perspective, and, of course, Kingston from an Asian American perspective. Each writer brings to bear a different historical experience of American racial discrimination: the African American experience of slavery, the Native American experience of dispossession and genocide, and the Chinese American experience of immigration have shaped quite different cultural responses to mainstream American society. Morrison and Silko were with Kingston in a group of writers who visited China in 1984. At that time Kingston felt an affinity with them as people, but she has also described their writing as sharing significant similarities with hers: "There is so much human emotion and richness and story and imagery and colors and things to eat. Nobody is alienated from life; everybody is warm. I feel that we write like that because we are warm, even though we all—I hate to say master—we are all very good with words, words aren't the only thing that's important. We care about stories about people, and also that magical real place that we are all visiting."[21]

Kingston, like Morrison in *Song of Solomon* (1977) and Silko in *Ceremony* (1977), uses myth, legend, dreams, and folklore. She reports that Morrison has tried to work out the reasons for the similarities between their styles of writing: "When we've talked about our backgrounds in myth and storytelling, it sounds like we grew up in very similar ways. Toni was trying to figure out where we belong, and she kept using that term 'magical realism'; she thought we were in that tradition."[22] The term *magical realism* describes a style of writing in which no distinction is made between realistic and fantastic events and circumstances. In *Song of Solomon,* for example, Morrison creates a character who is born without a navel; then, in the conclusion of the narrative, the protagonist, Milkman Dead, realizes in his physical actions the mythical feats of a slave who leaps all the way back to Africa. The blending of extraordinary details such as these into the texture of the realistic narrative is comparable with such episodes in *The Woman Warrior* as the one in which Brave Orchid wrestles with a ghost as if it were a real person and the one in which she assists in the birth of a baby who has no anus.

Kingston contrasts the quality of this style of writing, which, in her words, arises from a sense of "connection with people who have a community and a tribe," with the style of mainstream post-modernist fiction.[23] While her writing shares some of the qualities of self-reflexivity, playfulness, indeterminacy, and ambiguity that characterize the postmodern fiction of writers such as Thomas Pynchon, John Barth, and Kurt Vonnegut, Kingston distances herself from them and from the entire movement of literary postmodernism. In the essay "*The Woman Warrior* as Postmodern Autobiography," however, Marilyn Yalom argues that Kingston's writing shares significant stylistic similarities with postmodernist fiction and that her work is "at the vortex of the most vital and innovative literary currents of the late twentieth century." Among the qualities that Yalom sees as characteristic of postmodernist fiction are "openness, pluralism, marginality, difference, discontinuity, incoherence, fragmentation, absence, skepticism, irony, playfulness, ambiguity, chance, popular culture, heterogeneity, circularity, and 'polymorphous' diffusion, in contrast to their opposites (closed systems, single authority, centeredness, sameness, continuity, coherence, wholeness, presence, certainty, sincerity, seriousness, design, high culture, hierarchy, and 'phallic' linearity)."[24] This opposition, Yalom observes, is helpful in distinguishing postmodernist writers—among whom she counts Barth, Pynchon, John Fowles, and E. L. Doctorow, along with Kingston—from their modernist predecessors, such as Katherine Anne Porter and Ernest Hemingway, and from contemporary writers who work more conventionally within the American literary canon, such as John Updike and Anne Tyler.

Seen in these terms, Kingston's work upsets the order and coherence of traditional autobiography by decentering the protagonist and presenting her obliquely through a series of alter egos who are presented through myth, talk-story, recollection, ballads, tales, and legends, all of which are mediated through the figure of the mother who originally told them to the narrator. In this way Kingston shatters the certainties upon which traditional autobiography is constructed and in its place creates a postmodernist form built upon the principles of indirection and ambiguity. Yalom attributes this stylistic innovation to Kingston's adoption of a postmodernist aesthetic: "Kingston's skepticism regarding the value of fixed endings and final truths, her delight in ironic twists and unforeseen peripeteia, are expressions of a distinctly postmodern sensibility."[25] Yalom sees this postmodernist quality extending from *The Woman Warrior* into the autobiographical writing of *China Men* but also influencing the style of *Tripmaster Monkey*. Kingston's use of the anarchic trickster figure of the Monkey King not only underscores the playful, indeterminate, postmodern nature of the novel, but her use of the trickster has also been linked to the representation of this mythical figure in the work of other ethnic writers, most notably the Native American writer Gerald Vizenor and the African American Ishmael Reed.[26]

In her discussion of the postmodernist quality of *Tripmaster Monkey,* "Clashing Constructs of Reality: Reading Maxine Hong Kingston's *Tripmaster Monkey* as Indigenous Ethnography," Patricia Lin compares Wittman's desire to stage the play *Shui Hu Chuan* with Jorge Luis Borges's story "Pierre Menard, the Author of *Don Quixote*" (1939). In both texts the protagonist chooses to repeat or reenact an existing literary text rather than create something new and unique. Wittman and Menard achieve the erasure of the original authors—Cervantes in Menard's case and Lo Kuan Chung in Wittman's—by placing in the foreground their own reenactment or "faking" of the original text. Lin argues that in Kingston's novel and Borges's story, "the underlying message is that since claiming authorial authority over one's own life is an impossibility, the only artistic and hence independent claim that either Wittman or Menard can achieve is through their visibly proclaimed presences in the reenactment of prior discursive voices."[27] In the postmodern world originality is impossible because all thought is determined by what has been thought and written before; only the artifice of repetition and reenactment will allow the expression of individual creativity. Not only Wittman but Kingston herself is involved in this process of "faking," according to Lin. *Tripmaster Monkey* is a repetition of existing literary and cultural constructs. Kingston's text reenacts legends, stories, elements of popular culture both Western and Chinese and is, in this sense, a "fake book," as the subtitle of the novel (*His Fake Book*) suggests. Comparison of the novel with a postmodernist story such as Borges's makes clear the operation of faking and its significance for what Lin argues is Kingston's postmodernist aesthetic.

NOTES

1. Sidonie Smith, *A Poetics of Women's Autobiography: Marginality and the Fictions of Self-Representation* (Bloomington & Indianapolis: Indiana University Press, 1987), pp. 150–151.

2. Sau-ling Cynthia Wong, "Autobiography as Guided Chinatown Tour? Maxine Hong Kingston's *The Woman Warrior* and the Chinese American Autobiographical Controversy," in *Maxine Hong Kingston's The Woman Warrior: A Casebook,* edited by Wong (New York & Oxford: Oxford University Press, 1999), p. 37.

3. Ibid., p. 38.

4. Joan Lidoff, "Autobiography in a Different Voice: *The Woman Warrior* and the Question of Genre," in *Approaches to Teaching Kingston's The Woman Warrior,* edited by Shirley Geok-lin Lim (New York: Modern Language Association, 1991), p. 117.

5. Shirley K. Rose, "Metaphors and Myths of Cross-Cultural Literacy: Autobiographical Narratives by Maxine Hong Kingston, Richard Rodriguez, and Malcolm X," *MELUS,* 14, no. 1 (1987): 4.

6. Ibid., p. 14.

7. Amy Ling, "Chinamerican Women Writers: Four Forerunners of Maxine Hong Kingston," in Gender/Body/Knowledge: Feminist Reconstructions of Being and Knowing, edited by Alison Jaggar and Susan Bordo (New Brunswick, N.J.: Rutgers University Press, 1989), p. 319.

8. Huang Chua, *Crossings* (Boston: Northeastern University Press, 1986), p. 122.

9. Patricia Lin Blinde, "The Icicle in the Desert: Perspective and Form in the Works of Two Chinese-American Women Writers," *MELUS,* 6, no. 3 (1979): 59.

10. Ling, *Between Worlds: Women Writers of Chinese Ancestry* (New York & Oxford: Pergamon Press, 1990), p. 120.

11. Ibid., p. 120.

12. Ibid., p. 130.

13. Ibid., p. 133.

14. Ibid., p. 141.

15. Shirley Geok-lin Lim, "Twelve Asian American Writers: In Search of Self-Definition," in *Redefining American Literary History,* edited by A. LaVonne Brown Ruoff and Jerry W. Ward (New York: Modern Language Association, 1990), p. 237.

16. Ibid., p. 238.

17. Jeanne R. Smith, "Rethinking American Culture: Maxine Hong Kingston's *Tripmaster Monkey,*" *Modern Language Studies,* 26 (Fall 1996): 71.

18. King-Kok Cheung, "'Don't Tell': Imposed Silences in *The Color Purple* and *The Woman Warrior,*" in *Reading the Literatures of Asian America,* edited by Lim and Ling (Philadelphia: Temple University Press, 1992), p. 163.

19. Ibid., p. 165.

20. David Leiwei Li, "The Production of Chinese American Tradition: Displacing American Orientalist Discourse," in *Reading the Literatures of Asian America,* p. 323.

21. Paula Rabinowitz, "Eccentric Memories: A Conversation with Maxine Hong Kingston," in *Conversations with Maxine Hong Kingston,* edited by Paul Skenazy and Tera Martin (Jackson: University Press of Mississippi, 1998), p. 74.

22. Jody Hoy, "To Be Able to See the Tao," in *Conversations with Maxine Hong Kingston,* p. 54.

23. Rabinowitz, "Eccentric Memories: A Conversation with Maxine Hong Kingston," p. 74.

24. Marilyn Yalom, "*The Woman Warrior* as Postmodern Autobiography," in *Approaches to Teaching Kingston's The Woman Warrior,* pp. 108–109.

25. Ibid., p. 113.

26. See John Lowe, "Monkey Kings and Mojo: Postmodern Ethnic Humor in Kingston, Reed, and Vizenor," *MELUS,* 21 (Winter 1996): 103–126.

27. Patricia Lin, "Clashing Constructs of Reality: Reading Maxine Hong Kingston's *Tripmaster Monkey* as Indigenous Ethnography," in *Reading the Literatures of Asian America,* p. 342.

RESOURCES FOR STUDY OF
MAXINE HONG KINGSTON

STUDY QUESTIONS

1. Why is Kingston's use of traditional Chinese myth considered controversial by some Asian American critics?

2. In what ways is Kingston's autobiographical form innovative?

3. What is meant by the term "double consciousness"? How can this term be applied to Kingston's writing?

4. Explore the parallels between the historical treatment of Chinese immigrants in America and Kingston's representation of the immigrant experience.

5. Analyze Kingston's use of narrative voice. Why does she invariably use a feminine narrator?

6. Kingston describes *The Woman Warrior* and *China Men* as originally comprising one single long book. Discuss the formal and thematic relations between the two narratives.

7. Consider the treatment of mother-daughter relationships in the work of Kingston and Amy Tan.

8. Kingston has remarked that, given the kind of upbringing she experienced, there was never any question but that she would be a feminist. Analyze the consequences for her writing of her feminist commitment.

9. Using examples from *The Woman Warrior* and *China Men,* illustrate what is meant by the terms patriarchy and misogyny.

10. The figure of the woman warrior seeks to forge a reconciliation of East and West; Kingston represents her achievement as having "conquered both North America and Asia." In what way can this figure be seen as symbolic of her mission as a writer?

11. Discuss the significance of the image of the stage and the idea of acting in Kingston's work.

12. Analyze Kingston's depiction of madness. Does her treatment of madness differ according to whether she is describing female as opposed to male madness?

13. Some critics have described Kingston's achievement as the development of a self-conscious and self-reflexive narrative style. Consider the self-reflexive qualities of her novel, *Tripmaster Monkey*, in relation to the earlier autobiographical works.

14. Find as many examples as you can of what Kingston calls her "American language with a Chinese accent."

15. Analyze the importance of geographical setting—Stockton, San Francisco, Hawaii, New York, Alaska, and China—in Kingston's work.

16. Consider the relationship between the theme of cross-cultural identity and the image of cross-racial marriage in *Tripmaster Monkey*.

17. What kind of humor does Kingston use in her writing? How has her use of humor changed as her writing career has developed?

18. Kingston refuses to be considered a "representative" Chinese American writer, insisting that she writes from her experience of her family and the small village in southern China from which they emigrated. How does she refuse the tag of "representative writer" or "spokesperson" in her literary work?

19. Consider the impact of Kingston's years of student protest upon her writing.

20. Kingston followed her antiwar protests with years of working in various ways with Vietnam veterans. How does the image of the Vietnam War enter into her writing?

21. Analyze the imagery of war in Kingston's writing. How does she reconcile this martial imagery with her avowed commitment to peace?

22. Kingston has described the importance to her work of the operations of memory, which sifts the important from the unimportant and presents her with the materials for her work. How does memory function as a structural device in her writing?

23. Compare Kingston's autobiographical writing in either *The Woman Warrior* or *China Men* with one other autobiographical work with which you are familiar. You should attend especially to such characteristics as the autobiographical subject, narrative voice, chronological structure, imagery, and tone.

24. Kingston variously describes the genre of her writing as autobiography, biography, and fiction. Place her work within one of these genres, demonstrating the connection between the characteristics of the genre and her literary practice.

25. What qualities does Kingston's work share with that of other prominent Asian American writers?

26. Compare the theme of silence in *The Woman Warrior* and Alice Walker's *The Color Purple*.

27. Kingston has drawn parallels between Frank Chin's attack on her representation of patriarchal Chinese culture and Ishmael Reed's attack on Alice Walker's depiction of African American male violence. Compare Kingston's refusal to create a sanitized version of ethnic culture with a similar refusal by other women writers of color.

28. Analyze the treatment of storytelling in the work of Kingston, Leslie Marmon Silko, and Toni Morrison.

29. Compare the use of the trickster figure in the work of Kingston, Gerald Vizenor, and Ishmael Reed. How does the difference in ethnic context (Chinese American, Native American, and African American, respectively) influence the representation of the trickster?

30. In what ways can Kingston's writing be termed "political"? Attend to her characters' sense of personal politics as well as her own comments on this subject.

GLOSSARY OF TERMS

Autobiography. The story of the life of a person, told by that person. An autobiography is assumed to be based upon fact, rather than invention, and to present a full account of the personal history of the subject. Usually included is an account of the activities, personality, and achievements of the subject, as well as an indication of the social, political, artistic, and historical milieu in which he or she lived. In contrast to autobiography, a memoir places emphasis upon the people the subject has known and the historical events witnessed. A diary or journal is a daily record of the subject's thoughts and experiences, which is written for personal reasons and not specifically for publication.

Bildungsroman. A novel of development, telling the story of an individual's developing character from earliest childhood through various experiences to maturity. The narrative ends with the beginning of adult life and the recognition of the protagonist's role in the world.

Episodic narrative. A narrative that consists of a series of incidents or episodes. Each episode possesses its own unity or coherence and is loosely connected to the others by a single narrative device or motif, such as a journey or quest.

Epistolary novel. A novel in which the narrative is wholly presented in the form of letters written by one or more of the characters.

Feminism. A politically based movement concerned with the liberation of women from male oppression and feminine marginalization. Feminists are committed to reforming societies that are seen to be based upon the interests of men. Feminism seeks to expose the cultural practices and attitudes that create an imbalance of power and to transform those power relationships into relations of equality between men and women.

Imagery. The pictorial elements of a literary work, or, more broadly, those elements that evoke a sensory perception in the reader. Imagery also refers to the instances of figurative language used in a literary text, such as metaphors and similes, to generate particular meanings and effects.

Juxtaposition. Close physical contrast or comparison between two elements in a narrative.

Kunstlerroman. A subtype of the bildungsroman, a kind of narrative that tells the story of a young artist's development to maturity, beginning with his or her earliest memories and ending with the realization of his or her artistic destiny.

Misogyny. Woman-hating; the term refers to a set of social and cultural practices that enforce the inferior position of women in a society.

Myth. A story about supernatural beings, once believed to be true by a particular cultural group, which explains the operations of nature or the establishment of social customs and rituals.

Narrator. A character who tells the story. Narrators vary in their level of knowledge about the events and people in the story; they can tell only what they see or know. Third-person narratives are often told from a perspective that is omniscient, or knowledgeable about every aspect of the story, but they may be limited as well.

Patriarchy. A society governed by men and structured to serve the interests of men. In a patriarchy women are excluded from positions of influence and are kept in a position of powerlessness relative to men.

Plot. The structure of actions or sequence of events that comprise a narrative. The ordering of action to produce particular effects produces the plot of a text.

Point of view. The way in which a story is told; how the reader is introduced to characters and actions in a narrative. The point of view describes the relation of the narrator to the narrative being told. An omniscient narrator knows everything there is to be known about the characters and events of the narrative, is able to move freely in time and space, and has privileged insight into the characters' motivations, thoughts, and feelings, which may or may not be revealed to the reader. A narrator with a limited point of view has access to the experience, thoughts, and feelings of a single character or a small group of characters in the narrative.

Setting. The location and historical period within which the narrative action takes place.

BIBLIOGRAPHY

BASIC REFERENCE WORKS

Lim, Shirley Geok-lin, ed. *Approaches to Teaching Kingston's The Woman Warrior.* New York: Modern Language Association, 1991. A collection of essays with a pedagogical bias; includes a personal statement by Kingston and useful discussions of her formal experimentation, her use of traditional Chinese sources, and ways of approaching the text in the classroom.

Simmons, Diane. *Maxine Hong Kingston.* New York: Twayne, 1999. A comprehensive account of Kingston's work. Simmons includes an extensive biographical essay and a brief interview with the author as well as close textual analyses of *The Woman Warrior, China Men,* and *Tripmaster Monkey.*

Wong, Sau-ling Cynthia, ed. *Maxine Hong Kingston's The Woman Warrior: A Casebook.* New York & Oxford: Oxford University Press, 1999. A useful collection representing the characteristic approaches to the text and the historical development of criticism of the book.

INTERVIEWS

Brownmiller, Susan. "Susan Brownmiller Talks with Maxine Hong Kingston." *Mademoiselle* (March 1977): 148–149, 210–211, 214–216.

Carabi, Angeles. "Interview with Maxine Hong Kingston." *Belles Lettres* (Winter 1989): 10–11.

Moyers, Bill. *A Conversation with Maxine Hong Kingston* (videocassette). Alexandria, Va.: Public Broadcasting Service/Public Affairs Television, 1990.

Skenazy, Paul, and Tera Martin, eds. *Conversations with Maxine Hong Kingston.* Jackson: University Press of Mississippi, 1998. Brings together sixteen interviews, with an introduction by the editors and a chronology of Kingston's life and career.

Thompson, Phyllis Hoge, "This Is the Story I Heard: A Conversation with Maxine Hong Kingston and Earll Kingston." *Biography,* 6 (Winter 1983): 1–12.

ASIAN AMERICAN LITERATURE

Chen, Victoria. "Chinese American Women, Language, and Moving Subjectivity." *Women and Language,* 18 (Spring 1995): 3–7.

Hattori, Tomo. "China Man Autoeroticism and the Remains of Asian America." *Novel,* 31 (Spring 1998): 215–236.

Hune, Shirley, Hyung Chan Kim, Stephen S. Fugita, and Amy Ling, eds. *Asian Americans: Comparative and Global Perspectives.* Pullman: Washington State University Press, 1991.

Kingston. "The Coming Book." In *The Writer on Her Work,* edited by Janet Sternberg. New York: Norton, 1980.

Kingston. "Cultural Mis-readings by American Reviewers." In *Asian and Western Writers in Dialogue: New Cultural Identities,* edited by Guy Amirthanayagam. London: Macmillan, 1982.

Kingston. "Finding a Voice." In *Language: Readings in Language and Culture,* edited by Virginia P. Clark, Paul A. Eschholz, and Alfred F. Rosa, New York: St. Martin's Press, 1998.

Kingston. "How Are You? I Am Fine, Thank You. And You?" In *The State of the Language,* edited by Christopher Ricks and Leonard Michaels. Berkeley: University of California Press, 1980.

Kingston. "The Novel's Next Step: From the Novel of the Americas to the Global Novel." In *The Novel in the Americas,* edited by Raymond Leslie Williams. Niwot: University Press of Colorado, 1992.

Kingston. "Postscript as Process." In *The Bedford Reader,* edited by X. J. Kennedy and Dorothy M. Kennedy. New York: Bedford Books, 1985.

Kingston. "Precepts for the Twentieth Century." In Thich Nhát-Hanh, *For a Future to be Possible: Commentaries on the Five Wonderful Precepts.* Berkeley: Parallax Press, 1993.

Kingston. "Reservations About China." *Ms.* (October 1978): 67–79.

Kingston. "San Francisco's Chinatown: A View from the Other Side of Arnold Genthe's Camera." *American Heritage,* 30 (December 1978): 36–47.

Kingston and Thich Nhát-Hanh. "Forward." In Chân Khõng Cao Ngoc Phuong, *Learning True Love: How I Learned and Practiced Social Change in Vietnam.* Berkeley: Parallax Press, 1993.

Lim, Shirley Geok-lin, and Amy Ling, eds. *Reading the Literatures of Asian America.* Philadelphia: Temple University Press, 1992.

Ling. *Between Worlds: Women Writers of Chinese Ancestry.* New York & Oxford: Pergamon Press, 1990.

Ling. "Chinamerican Women Writers: Four Forerunners of Maxine Hong Kingston." In *Gender/Body/Knowledge: Feminist Reconstructions of Being and Knowing,* edited by Alison Jaggar and Susan Bordo. New Brunswick: Rutgers University Press, 1989.

Ling. "Chinese American Women Writers: The Tradition behind Maxine Hong Kingston." In *Redefining American Literary History,* edited by A. LaVonne Brown Ruoff and Jerry W. Ward. New York: Modern Language Association, 1990.

Ling, Jinqi. "Identity Crisis and Gender Politics: Reappropriating Asian American Masculinity." In *An Interethnic Companion to Asian American Literature,* edited by King-Kok Cheung. Cambridge: Cambridge University Press, 1997.

CRITICAL STUDIES

Blinde, Patricia Lin. "The Icicle in the Desert: Perspective and Form in the Works of Two Chinese-American Women Writers." *MELUS,* 6, no. 3 (1979): 51–71. Discusses the autobiographical work of Kingston and Jade Snow Wong.

Buss, Helen M. "Memoir with an Attitude: One Reader Reads *The Woman Warrior: Memoirs of a Girlhood among Ghosts.*" *A-B: Auto-Biography Studies,* 12 (Fall 1997): 203–224.

Castillo, Debra A. "The Daily Shape of Horses: Denise Chávez and Maxine Hong Kingston." *Dispositio,* 16, no. 4 (1991): 29–43.

Chang, Hsiao-Hung. "Gender Crossing in Maxine Hong Kingston's *Tripmaster.*" *MELUS,* 22 (Spring 1997): 15–34.

Cheung, Kai-Chong. "Maxine Hong Kingston's Non-Chinese Man." *Tamkang Review,* 23 (Fall 1992 – Summer 1993): 421–430.

Cheung, King-Kok. *Articulate Silences: Hisaye Yamamoto, Maxine Hong Kingston, Joy Kogawa.* Ithaca: Cornell University Press, 1993. Places Kingston within the context of significant Asian American women writers.

Cheung. "Self-Fulfilling Visions in *The Woman Warrior* and *Thousand Pieces of Gold.*" *Biography,* 13 (Spring 1990): 143–153.

Cheung. "Talk Story: Counter-Memory in Maxine Hong Kingston's *China Men.*" *Tamkang Review,* 24 (Fall 1993): 21–37.

Chu, Patricia P. "*Tripmaster Monkey,* Frank Chin, and the Chinese Heroic Tradition." *Arizona Quarterly,* 53 (Autumn 1997): 117–139. A discussion of the controversy between Kingston and Frank Chin over how the canon of Chinese American literature should be characterized.

Chun, Gloria. "The High Note of the Barbarian Reed Pipe: Maxine Hong Kingston." *Journal of Ethnic Studies,* 19 (Fall 1991): 85–94.

Cliff, Michele. "The Making of Americans: Maxine Hong Kingston's Crossover Dreams." *Village Voice Literary Supplement,* 74 (May 1989): 11–13.

Cook, Rufus. "Maintaining the Past: Cultural Continuity in Maxine Hong Kingston's Work." *Tamkang Review,* 25 (Fall 1994): 35–58.

Dasenbrock, Reed Way. "Intelligibility and Meaningfulness in Multicultural Literature in English." *PMLA,* 102 (January 1987): 10–19. Discusses Kingston's *The Woman Warrior,* along with R. K. Narayan's *The Painter of Signs* (1976), Rudolfo Anaya's *Bless Me, Ultima* (1972), and Witi Ihimaera's *Tangi* (1973), as texts that demonstrate both "implicit" as well as "explicit" multicultural features.

Deeney, John J. "Of Monkeys and Butterflies: Transformation in M. H. Kingston's *Tripmaster Monkey* and D. H. Hwang's *M. Butterfly,*" *MELUS,* 18 (Winter 1993–1994): 21–39.

Donaldson, Mara E. "Woman as Hero in Margaret Atwood's *Surfacing* and Maxine Hong Kingston's *The Woman Warrior.*" In *Heroines of Popular Culture,* edited by Pat Browne. Bowling Green, Ohio: Bowling Green State University Popular Press, 1987.

Eakin, Paul John. *Fictions in Autobiography: Studies in the Art of Self-Invention.* Princeton: Princeton University Press, 1985. A relatively early discussion of Kingston's innovative use of the autobiographical form within a generic context.

Fong, Bobby. "Maxine Hong Kingston's Autobiographical Strategy in *The Woman Warrior.*" *Biography,* 12 (Spring 1989): 116–126.

Friedman, Susan Stanford. "Women's Autobiographical Selves: Theory and Practice." In *The Private Self: Theory and Practice of Women's Autobiographical Writings,* edited by Shari Benstock. Chapel Hill: University of North Carolina Press, 1988.

Frye, Joanne S. "*The Woman Warrior:* Claiming Narrative Power, Recreating Female Selfhood." In *Faith of a (Woman) Writer,* edited by Alice Kessler Harris and William McBrien. Westport, Conn.: Greenwood Press, 1988.

Furth, Isabella. "Beee-e-een! Nation, Transformation, and the Hyphen of Ethnicity in Kingston's *Tripmaster Monkey.*" *Modern Fiction Studies,* 40 (Spring 1994): 33–49.

Hayes, Daniel. "Autobiography's Secret." *A-B: Auto-Biography Studies,* 12 (Fall 1997): 243–260.

Henke, Suzette A. "Women's Life-Writing and the Minority Voice: Maya Angelou, Maxine Hong Kingston, and Alice Walker." In *Traditions, Voices, and Dreams: The American*

Novel since the 1960s, edited by Melvin J. Friedman and Ben Siegel. Newark: University of Delaware Press, 1995.

Hunt, Linda. "'I could not figure out what was my village': Gender vs. Ethnicity in Maxine Hong Kingston's *The Woman Warrior.*" *MELUS,* 12 (Fall 1985): 5–12. A discussion of the interplay between racial and gender issues.

Juhasz, Suzanne. "Maxine Hong Kingston: Narrative Technique and Female Identity." In *Contemporary American Women Writers: Narrative Strategies,* edited by Catherine Rainwater and William J. Scheick. Lexington: University Press of Kentucky, 1985. Analysis of Kingston's narrative technique in *The Woman Warrior* and *China Men.*

Lappas, Catherine. "'The Way I Heard It Was . . .': Myth, Memory, and Autobiography in *Storyteller* and *The Woman Warrior.*" *CEA Critic,* 57 (Fall 1994): 57–67. A comparative discussion of Kingston and the Native American writer Leslie Marmon Silko.

Lee, Rachel. "Claiming Land, Claiming Voice, Claiming Canon: Institutionalized Challenges in Kingston's *China Men* and *The Woman Warrior.*" In *Reviewing Asian America: Locating Diversity,* edited by Wendy L. Ng, Soo Young Chin, James S. Moy, and Gary Y. Okihiro. Pullman: Washington State University Press, 1995.

Lee, Robert A. "Ethnic Renaissance: Rudolfo Anaya, Louise Erdrich, and Maxine Hong Kingston." In *The New American Writing: Essays on American Literature Since 1970,* edited by Graham Clarke. New York: St. Martin's Press, 1990.

Li, David Leiwei. "*China Men:* Maxine Hong Kingston and the American Canon." *American Literary History,* 2 (Fall 1990): 482–502.

Li. "The Naming of a Chinese American 'I': Cross-Cultural Sign/ifications in *The Woman Warrior.*" *Criticism,* 30 (Fall 1988): 497–515.

Lidoff, Joan. "Autobiography in a Different Voice: Maxine Hong Kingston's *The Woman Warrior.*" *A-B: Auto-Biography Studies,* 3 (Fall 1987): 29–35.

Ling, Amy. "Maxine Hong Kingston and the Dialogic Dilemma of Asian American Writers." *Bucknell Review,* 39 (1995): 151–166.

Ling. "Thematic Threads in Maxine Hong Kingston's *The Woman Warrior.*" *Tamkang Review,* 14 (Autumn 1983 – Summer 1984): 155–164.

Linton, Patricia. "'What Stories the Wind Would Tell': Representation and Appropriation in Maxine Hong Kingston's *China Men.*" *MELUS,* 19 (Winter 1994): 37–48.

Lowe, John. "Monkey Kings and Mojo: Postmodern Ethnic Humor in Kingston, Reed, and Vizenor." *MELUS,* 21 (Winter 1996): 103–126.

Madsen, Deborah L. "(Dis)Figuration: The Body as Icon in the Writings of Maxine Hong Kingston." *Yearbook of English Studies,* 24 (1994): 237–250.

Martinez, Sharon Suzuki. "Trickster Strategies: Challenging American Identity, Community, and Art in Kingston's *Tripmaster Monkey.*" In *Reviewing Asian America.*

Melchior, Bonnie. "A Marginal 'I': The Autobiographical Self Deconstructed in Maxine Hong Kingston's *The Woman Warrior.*" *Biography,* 17 (Summer 1994): 281–295.

Miller, Margaret. "Threads of Identity in Maxine Hong Kingston's *Woman Warrior.*" *Biography,* 6 (Winter 1983): 13–33.

Mitchell, Carol. "'Talking Story' in *The Woman Warrior:* An Analysis of the Use of Folklore." *Kentucky Folklore Record,* 27 (January–June 1981): 5–12.

Morante, Linda. "From Silence to Song: The Triumph of Maxine Hong Kingston." *Frontiers,* 9, no. 2 (1987): 78–82.

Neubauer, Carol E. "Developing Ties to the Past: Photography and Other Sources of Information in Maxine Hong Kingston's *China Men.*" *MELUS,* 10 (Winter 1983): 17–36.

Nishime, LeiLana. "Engendering Genre: Gender and Nationalism in *China Men* and *The Woman Warrior.*" *MELUS,* 20 (Spring 1995): 67–82.

Ordonez, Elizabeth J. "Narrative Texts by Ethnic Women: Rereading the Past, Reshaping the Future." *MELUS,* 9 (Winter 1982): 19–28.

Outka, Paul. "Publish or Perish: Food, Hunger, and Self-Construction in Maxine Hong Kingston's *The Woman Warrior.*" *Contemporary Literature,* 38 (Fall 1997): 447–482.

Rabine, Leslie W. "No Lost Paradise: Social Gender and Symbolic Gender in the Writings of Maxine Hong Kingston." *Signs,* 12 (Spring 1987): 471–492. Uses French feminist theory to distinguish between gender as a system of social relations and gender as an effect of discourse and applies these ideas to Kingston's representation of gender.

Rolf, Robert. "On Maxine Hong Kingston and *The Woman Warrior.*" *Kyushu American Literature,* 23 (May 1982): 1–10.

Rose, Shirley K. "Metaphors and Myths of Cross-Cultural Literacy: Autobiographical Narratives by Maxine Hong Kingston, Richard Rodriguez, and Malcolm X." *MELUS,* 14 (Spring 1987): 3–15.

Sato, Gayle K. Fujita. "Ghosts as Chinese-American Constructs in Maxine Hong Kingston's *The Woman Warrior.*" In *Haunting the House of Fiction: Feminist Perspectives on Ghost Stories by American Women,* edited by Lynette Carpenter and Wendy K. Kolmar. Knoxville: University of Tennessee Press, 1991.

Schueller, Malini. "Questioning Race and Gender Definitions: Dialogic Subversions in *The Woman Warrior.*" *Criticism,* 31 (Fall 1989): 421–437.

Schueller. "Theorizing Ethnicity and Subjectivity: Maxine Hong Kingston's *Tripmaster Monkey* and Amy Tan's *The Joy Luck Club.*" *Genders,* 15 (Winter 1992): 72–85.

Shan, Te Hsing. "Law as Literature, Literature as Law: Articulating 'The Laws' in Maxine Hong Kinston's *China Men.*" *Tamkang Review,* 26 (Autumn–Winter 1995): 235–264.

Shih, Shu Mei. "Exile and Intertextuality in Maxine Hong Kingston's *China Men.*" In *The Literature of Emigration and Exile,* edited by James Whitlark and Wendell Aycock. Lubbock: Texas Tech University Press, 1992.

Shostak, Debra. "Maxine Hong Kingston's Fake Books." In *Memory, Narrative, and Identity: New Essays in Ethnic American Literatures,* edited by Amritjit Singh, Joseph T. Skerrett Jr., and Robert E. Hogan. Boston: Northeastern University Press, 1994.

Skenazy, Paul. "Replaying Time." *Enclitic,* 11, no. 3 (1989): 36–42. A discussion of *Tripmaster Monkey* in which Skenazy points out that Kingston's skill as a writer is sometimes obscured by the attention paid to her racial and gender themes.

Sledge, Linda Ching. "Oral Tradition in Kingston's *China Men.*" In *Redefining American Literary History,* edited by A. LaVonne Brown Ruoff and Jerry W. Ward. New York: Modern Language Association, 1990.

Smith, Jeanne R. "Rethinking American Culture: Maxine Hong Kingston's Cross-Cultural *Tripmaster Monkey.*" *Modern Language Studies,* 26 (Fall 1996): 71–81.

Tanner, James T. F. "Walt Whitman's Presence in Maxine Hong Kingston's *Tripmaster Monkey: His Fake Book,*" *MELUS,* 20 (Winter 1995): 61–74.

Wang, Alfred S. "Maxine Hong Kingston's Reclaiming of America: The Birthright of the Chinese American Male." *South Dakota Review,* 26 (Spring 1988): 18–29.

Wang, Jennie. "*Tripmaster Monkey:* Kingston's Postmodern Representation of a

New 'China Man.'" *MELUS,* 20 (Spring 1995): 101–114.

Wang, Veronica. "Reality and Fantasy: The Chinese-American Woman's Quest for Identity." *MELUS,* 12 (Fall 1985): 23–31.

Williams, A. Noelle. "Parody and Pacifist Transformations in Maxine Hong Kingston's *Tripmaster Monkey: His Fake Book.*" *MELUS,* 20 (Spring 1995): 83–100.

Wong, Sau-ling Cynthia. "Necessity and Extravagance in Maxine Hong Kingston's *The Woman Warrior:* Art and the Ethnic Experience." *MELUS,* 15 (Spring 1988): 4–26.

Woo, Deborah. "Maxine Hong Kingston: The Ethnic Writer and the Burden of Dual Authenticity." *Amerasia Journal,* 16, no. 1 (1990): 173–200.

Wu, Qing Yun. "A Chinese Reader's Response to Maxine Hong Kingston's *China Men.*" *MELUS,* 17 (Fall 1991): 85–94.

Yu, Ning. "A Strategy against Marginalization: The 'High' and 'Low' Cultures in Kingston's *China Men.*" *College Literature,* 23 (October 1996): 73–87.

WEB SITES

"Maxine Hong Kingston." http://www.hmco.com/college/english/heath/syllabuild/iguide/kingston.html. This page, with text by Amy Ling, is found on the website of the publishing firm Houghton Mifflin. The page includes brief but useful entries on such topics as teaching strategies, themes in Kingston's work, and questions for reading and discussion.

"Maxine Hong Kingston Teacher Resource Guide." http://falcon.jmu.edu/schoollibrary/kingston.htm. A teacher resource guide from James Madison University; includes a Kingston biography and a series of lesson plans.

"Maxine Hong Kingston: Warrior Woman." http://www.cwrl.utexas.edu/~natasha/usauto_html/kingston/. An organization called the Kingston Group has created this site, which explores gender and feminism issues, autobiography, and the interpretation and critical reception of the work of ethnic authors, especially Kingston.

"Voices from the Gaps." http://voices.cla.umn.edu/authors/MaxineHongKingston.html. This site is a useful resource for information about a large range of ethnic writers. The Kingston page includes a biography, a list of her publications, a selection of critical works, and links to other sites of relevance.

SPECIAL COLLECTION

The Maxine Hong Kingston Papers, The Bancroft Library, University of California, Berkeley.

INDEX